Books by Sanaya Roman

Earth Life Series

Living With Joy:
Keys to Personal Power and Spiritual Transformation

Personal Power Through Awareness:
A Guidebook for Sensitive People

Spiritual Growth:
Being Your Higher Self

Soul Life Series

Soul Love:
Awakening Your Heart Centers

Books by Sanaya Roman and Duane Packer, Ph.D.

Opening to Channel:
How to Connect with Your Guide

Creating Money:
Keys to Abundance

KEYS TO ABUNDANCE

Sanaya Roman and Duane Packer

HJ Kramer Inc
Tiburon, California

H J Kramer Inc
P. O. Box 1082
Tiburon, California 94920

Library of Congress Cataloging-in-Publication Data

Roman, Sanaya.
    Creating money : keys to abundance / Sanaya Roman and Duane Packer. – 1st pbk. ed. – Tiburon, Calif. : H J Kramer, 1988
        xxx, 254 p. ; 22 cm. – (Life mastery series ; bk. 1)
        ISBN 0-915811-09-X (pbk.) : $12.95

    1. Success.   2. Money.   3. Channeling (Spiritualism)   I. Packer, Duane R.
II. Title.   III. Series.
BJ1611.2.R576   1988   131 – dc19   88-160518
                                                     AACR 2   MARC

Cover painting: "Temple of Inner Light"
© 1987 by Judith Cornell

First paperback edition 1988
Manufactured in the United States of America

20   19   18   17   16   15   14   13   12

To the spirit of abundance
that is in each of you.
May you recognize your greatness,
discover your path,
and make the contribution you came to make.

Orin and DaBen

To Our Readers

The books we publish are our contribution to an emerging world based on cooperation rather than on competition, on affirmation of the human spirit rather than on self-doubt, and on the certainty that all humanity is connected. Our goal is to touch as many lives as possible with a message of hope for a better world.

Hal and Linda Kramer, Publishers

Contents

Preface / xi
How to Use This Book / xiv
How to Use the Affirmations / xvi
Introduction by Orin and DaBen / xix

SECTION 1

Creating Money

1 You Are the Source / 3
2 Becoming Abundant / 17
3 Discovering What You Want / 27
4 Magnetizing What You Want / 37

SECTION 2

Developing Mastery

5 Following Your Inner Guidance / 59

6   Allowing Success / 71
7   Transforming Your Beliefs / 81
8   Letting Money Flow / 88
9   Coming Out of Survival   95
10 Trusting / 109
11 Miracles / 121

SECTION 3

Creating Your Life's Work

12 You Can Do What You Love / 129
13 Discovering Your Life's Work / 137
14 You Have What It Takes / 149
15 Believing in Yourself / 164
16 Trusting the Flow / 173
17 Moving to Your Higher Path / 181

SECTION 4

Having Money

18 Honoring Your Value and Worth / 195
19 Joy and Appreciation / 202
20 Giving and Receiving / 210
21 Clarity and Harmony / 222
22 Having Money / 230
23 Savings: Affirming Your Abundance / 240

Companion Books by Orin and DaBen / 254

Exercises

Learning to Relax, Focus, and Visualize / 14

Expressing a Higher Quality / 25

General Magnetizing / 43

Magnetizing a Person You Don't Yet Know / 47

Magnetizing a Number of People / 50

Group Magnetizing / 53

Linking Up with the Higher Forces / 68

Energizing a Symbol of Your Life's Work / 135

Preface

Sanaya *(pronounced Sah-nay-ah):* I have been using the spiritual principles of manifestation presented in this book for the last several years with many wonderful results. At the time I received this information, I was struggling to survive on a day-to-day level, and had asked Orin, my teacher in spirit, for guidance. I had been channeling Orin's guidance for many years and had received much valuable information on a variety of topics.

Orin suggested that he teach me about manifesting by giving classes, so that I as well as others could learn how to create forms, objects, and money in the physical world using the spiritual laws of abundance. These principles have worked to help me get Orin's and my work out to the world, do what I love for a living, and gain the confidence that comes from understanding how manifesting works.

Duane has used these principles too, as well as many energy techniques for manifesting given to him by his spirit guide, DaBen. While his career as a geologist/geophysicist had been rewarding, he wanted to start a new career teaching channeling, developing his clairvoyant sight, and empowering people in their growth through energy and bodywork. He used these principles to energize his life's work, draw to him the people he could empower and serve, manifest the tools he needed for his new career, and gain clarity about money.

This book is an expansion of the manuscript entitled *Creating Money,* which came from Orin's teachings about the spiritual laws of abundance. The original manuscript was distributed to members of Orin's classes and many others who heard about and requested it. The demand for both manuscript and classes grew so great that Duane and I gave many additional workshops on creating money, magnetism, and advanced techniques of manifesting. Orin's spiritual principles and DaBen's energy techniques when used together have proved so effective in helping people create money and abundance that we have combined them in this book.

Orin and DaBen feel that the ability to manifest—to take one's visions, dreams, hopes, and fantasies and make them real—is one of the most important skills people can learn to empower themselves and become greater lights to the world around them. They want to help people learn how to create money and other things they want as tools for aliveness and growth, and let go of anxiety, confusion, and guilt around money. They want to help people love, value, and honor their work. They want to help people learn how to trust and listen to their inner guidance, awaken to their greater potential, and gain the confidence that comes from knowing they can create whatever they want.

They feel there are many people who aren't doing their life's work because they don't know how to manifest the money or the tools they need, or they do not believe their paths or contributions are important. Orin and DaBen feel that the ability to create abundance will greatly add to people's ability to live rewarding and fulfilling lives.

We have taught these principles to many people with many different goals. Some were drawn to our classes because they had wanted something for many years that they had not been able to create, or wanted money to launch a project they had thought about for a long time. Some wanted money so they could change jobs, become self-employed, go to school, or travel. Many had worked in one field and wanted to find work or create a career for themselves in a new field that reflected their changing interests. They wondered how to create enough money to support themselves while they made that transition. Some simply wanted to learn how to create money so they could spend more time on their spiritual lives, or take time off to write and explore. Others had created money and found that it had not brought them the joy or peace they had expected.

As people used the exercises in this book and created results with them, we saw them change in marvelous ways. They developed a sense of confidence and trust in the universe. They discovered that manifestation was a process of growth and increasing aliveness. They learned to take responsibility for their lives. With the discovery that they could have what they wanted came the need for new levels of clarity about what they did want. As they got clear on what they wanted, they were able to draw it to them more easily.

We saw many people make successful career transitions, greatly increase their incomes, and let go of their anxiety and worry over money. Once they were able to attract some of the material things they wanted, their attention became even more focused on the service they had come to contribute to mankind.

As these people learned how to create their life's work and fill their spiritual and physical needs, they felt more and more in control of their lives. They were able to see that they had whatever they had because of their earlier choices and decisions, and that they could change their circumstances for the better if they wanted to. They no longer felt that they were at the mercy of vast forces beyond their control. They came to see that having what one wants is not a lucky break that happens to some and not to others, but that each person has the tools to create what they want. As their skill and clarity increased with time, they were able to draw to them more than they had ever thought possible.

Our own progress toward mastering abundance has been a wonderful process of growth and enlightenment. The more we work with the principles in this book, the more we learn about their richness and simplicity. We have found them to be simple when we get playful, creative, and imaginative. They become complex only when we over-analyze about whether or not we are doing the exercises "right." The best results come from having fun with the exercises and trusting that whatever is best for us will come.

Creating things within a specific time period has been one of the more challenging aspects of creating money and form, and we are constantly reminded that all things come in their proper time. We have discovered that when we get clear about what we want and then surrender and detach, letting any form work, the results are usually much better than what we have asked for. If things do not come when we expect them, we realize later that having them was not for our highest good at that time.

You may have come to this book to create money for something specific, to become financially independent, to discover your life's work, or to help launch a business or project. You may be in transition, knowing that something new is coming and wanting to draw it to you more rapidly. You may want more sales, clients, or a higher income. You may want to resolve many questions you have about money. Whatever your reasons for reading this book, you can use the principles you find here in any area of your life, for they are the universal principles of energy and abundance. You can draw to you whatever you want that will contribute to your higher good, tapping into the unlimited abundance of the universe.

How to Use This Book

Sanaya and Duane: This book is a course in manifesting and creating abundance in your life. Section 1, *Creating Money*, is a step-by-step guide to the art of manifesting. You will learn how to discover what you want, drawing things to you that will fulfill and satisfy you, that are even better than what you ask for. You will learn advanced techniques of manifesting and how to work with your own energy and the power of magnetism to draw things into your life in the fastest, easiest way possible.

The second section of this book, *Developing Mastery*, will help you learn to work with and move through any blocks you may have about allowing abundance into your life. The third section, *Creating Your Life's Work*, will help you learn to make money and create abundance through doing the things you love. You will learn many simple energy techniques to draw your ideal job to you, discover your life's work, and do what you love for a living. The fourth section, *Having Money*, is about having and increasing money and abundance in your life. You will learn how to create joy, peace, harmony, clarity, and self-love with your money, letting it flow and increase.

Most chapters in Sections 2, 3, and 4 end with a playsheet designed to help you gain mastery over the process of creating what you want. It is important to be in a relaxed, focused state of mind when you do the playsheets. Before you answer the questions, sit quietly, take a few deep breaths, relax your body, and begin to open your mind to new ideas and thoughts.

As you focus on these new ideas, you may find yourself discovering many of your beliefs, and even your resistances. If you find yourself resisting answering a certain question, you may have a "charge" around this idea and it may be the very area you will most benefit from "playing" with to develop your abundance potential. There are no right or wrong answers, only new ways of experiencing how you create your reality. You may want to write down or simply think out the answers to the playsheets. Writing them down helps bring the thoughts from your mind into the physical world, and can be one of the first steps of manifesting.

One way to use this book is to ask what area you will benefit from working on with money, and then open the book to any page. Use that chapter, page, or affirmation as a sign from your higher self about the specific area you could work on that would create a shift in your prosperity right now.

Before you start Chapter 1, get quiet and go within. Do you intend to have abundance? Are you ready to become prosperous, to have what you want, and for money to work for you? Decide right now that you can have what you want. Your intention to create money and abundance is the first step toward having them in your life.

How to Use the Affirmations

Sanaya and Duane: We have included many affirmations—set off in larger type—throughout the book for you to use to increase your prosperity. Affirmations are positive statements that help focus your awareness on your power and ability to create and have what you want. They are stated in the present tense, such as "I have unlimited abundance." Your thoughts create your reality, and as you say these positive statements to yourself you will begin to create them as true for you. These affirmations were designed by Orin and DaBen to open and expand your awareness of what you can have, to align you with your soul's wisdom, and to attune you with the unlimited abundance of the universe. As you say them to yourself, you will create positive, more abundant circumstances in your life.

Use only those affirmations that feel appropriate to you. It is important that the words feel comfortable to you and are aligned with who you are. Feel free to substitute other words that have a special meaning to you, for the power of affirmations is increased when the statements feel comfortable and meaningful. We encourage you to make up your own prosperity affirmations as well.

Most of the affirmations start with "I." We use "I" to refer to all of who you are: your greater self (also called your higher self, your soul, the part of you that is connected to the God-force or the God-within, or the deeper part of your being) as well as the ego and personality selves. Affirmations are more powerful when all the parts of you are aligned and working together for a common goal. You can substitute other words that feel right to you. For example, in the affirmation "I am the source of my abundance," you may want to say "God is my source," or "My connection to God is my source," or "My soul is the source of my abundance."

To create results your affirmations need to feel possible; if what you are saying feels impossible to create, the affirmation will not bring you the results you are affirming. For instance, saying "I now have one million dollars" will not create results for you if you don't believe you can have this sum. It may be better to start with the affirmation "My income is now increased by at least ten percent" and work up from there as you experience success in creating what you are affirming.

There are several ways to use the affirmations in this book. One is to flip through the book, read any affirmations that appeal to you, and then sit quietly, saying them to yourself over and over. There is much power in repetition. You will be reprogramming your subconscious mind to accept these thoughts as reality, and as it does it will create changes in your life to match this new inner reality. You may want to say the affirmation on your in-breath, imagining as you say it that you are taking the statement up to your higher self. Then imagine on your out-breath that you are releasing the affirmation into the outer world where it will become your reality.

You can tape-record these affirmations and listen to them. For your convenience, we have recorded the affirmations in this book on an audio-cassette tape and printed them on calling-card size cards. (Refer to *Additional Resources* in back of book for information.) You may want to write them out yourself and put them where you can see them frequently, especially those that have meaning for you.

*I*ntroduction

Greetings from Orin and DaBen!

We invite you to explore your connection to money and abundance and to learn to work with matter and substance in new ways. Money does not come just to special people, people with a given talent or an inborn skill. Within you lie all the answers and talents you need to create unlimited abundance for yourself, to have what you need both physically and spiritually in every area of your life.

You are a magnificent, powerful person, and you can learn to work with your energy to tap into the unlimited abundance of the universe. Creating money can be effortless, the natural outcome of the way you live, think, and act. You can draw anything you want to you; you can realize your fondest dreams. This book is a course in creating abundance as well as money, for creating money alone will not always bring you what you want.

We, Orin and DaBen, are beings of light. We exist in the higher dimensions. We are here as assistants and spiritual teachers to help you with your personal growth and awaken you to the higher aspects of yourself. We hope to add a new dimension to your thinking about money. We want to help you tap into the unlimited abundance that is all around you. We offer you the thoughts and ideas in this book as our gift of love. It may seem as if you have always known much of what we say. We encourage you to accept into your heart only those ideas and suggestions that ring true to the deepest part of your being, and let go of any that do not.

You may wonder how we, as guides, would know about the laws of money, for we do not live on the material plane. Money is energy, and energy exists in all realms. The spiritual laws of money are universal energy laws that create abundance: the principles of ebb and flow, unlimited thinking, giving and receiving, appreciation, honoring your worth, clear agreements, magnetism, and more.

Abundance means more than having quantities of things; it means having things that fulfill you as well. Money can be part of your abundance; money can make sense in your life. As you become more skilled at manifesting, you will learn to consciously choose what you want to create and then draw it to you. Situations and objects will come into your life simultaneously with your need for them. You can learn to master money rather than being mastered by it. Through your mastery you will also allow situations and objects to leave your life gently and easily when you no longer need them, creating room for the next things that will serve you. There will be a natural flow of money, people, and things into and out of your life and each will serve your higher purpose and appear at exactly the right time.

New times are coming. Humanity is awakening to superconscious reality, and people will be experiencing an opening and intensification of their higher nature. In the times that are coming, you will be stimulated to express your higher self (also called your soul, the deepest part of your being, or the God-within) in everything you create. You will want the place you live, the items you buy, your relationships, and your lifestyle to reflect your higher ideals and values. In the way you earn and spend money you will be seeking to express your higher qualities of love, well-being, happiness, peace, aliveness, and awareness of who you are deep within. These new times will bring with them a tremendous creativity and an influx of ideas.

The ways money may be made and held are changing. Money and abundance will flow in greater amounts, be easier to hold, and give you more joy when you follow the spiritual laws of money. You follow the spiritual laws of money when you do your life's work and honor and serve the higher good of others. You follow the spiritual laws when you cooperate rather than compete with others, making every energy and money exchange a winning situation for everyone involved. You follow the spiritual laws of money when the way you make, spend, or invest money does not harm the earth.

You can join the new energies and align with your higher self by acting on your feelings and moving with the current, learning when to be an active force and when to surrender. You can increase the flow of money, objects, and things you want into your life by operating with more clarity, joy, harmony, and integrity, trusting that everything that happens is for your higher good. As you identify and let go of old situations that no longer serve you, as you open to new opportunities, thoughts, perceptions, and feelings, you will allow the higher energy of your soul to flow through you. Then money and abundance will come to you naturally and easily, without effort or struggle. The things you will create can bring you growth, expansion, renewal, and aliveness.

Finding and creating your life's work will bring you more abundance than any other single action you can take. Your life's work will involve doing what you love to do and will in some way make a contribution to the greater good of mankind. Money will be a by-product of doing what you love and will flow effortlessly into your life, without even much thought.

Many of you shun the path of your greatest creativity, joy, and aliveness, thinking that you will not be able to make enough money from it. We want to help you believe that you can have an abundance of money doing what you love to do; we want you to recognize that you do not have to stay in jobs that do not serve you. We will help you look at how to make the transition between where you are now and where you want to be. We have devoted an entire section of this book to showing you how to create a vision of your path and draw to you your life's work. We will show you many energy techniques to activate your higher path.

Each one of you who is called to this book is on a path of accelerated personal growth and has much to offer mankind, whether or not you are aware of it. Now is the time to listen to your inner messages and discover the special work you came to do. Begin to put that work out to the world, for it is very much needed. As you serve and empower others, find your life's work, and do what you love rather than what you think will bring you money, you will become highly magnetic to money. These new times will provide you with many opportunities to discover and fulfill your life's purpose, supporting all your efforts to put your work out to the world. Even a small step toward your higher path will bring rich rewards and results.

You can learn to create what you want using energy and thought rather than physical effort, and produce results that go beyond anything you can create with physical effort alone. When you understand how energy works you can take only those actions that bring you the greatest results without wasted effort. We will teach you how to draw things to you by achieving a relaxed, focused state of mind and working with energy and magnetism. These techniques are powerful and they do work.

You do not need to be affected by the economy or manmade conditions. You can create your own personal economic environment of prosperity. If you are willing to listen to and take action on your inner guidance, you will do well no matter what the economy around you is doing. You are being sent all the guidance you need to have abundance and be well provided for during economic downturns. If people lose their jobs or a lot of money, it will only be because those things are not for their higher good; such events will change their lives in some way for the better. If anything is truly serving your higher good, it won't be taken away.

There are two kinds of laws of money you will want to follow to create and keep it. The spiritual laws can be used to attract money, and the money that comes will bring you your highest good. The man-made laws of money include financial planning, time management, cash flow management, marketing, taxes, and business planning. Learn whatever is appropriate to help you understand and work with the man-made laws of money as they now exist. We will not cover the man-made laws in this book, for they are explained well elsewhere. You can create money with the spiritual laws alone. However, it is good to be aware of the rules that your society has created around money so that you are also in harmony with those rules. It will take less of your energy to attract, save, and create more money if you are in harmony with both the spiritual and man-made laws of money.

Many of you are trying to reconcile the idea of being on a spiritual path with having money. You may want the money in your life to reflect your integrity, compassion, and love for others through the way you earn and spend it. You can have money and follow your spiritual principles. Money will come from attuning to your soul's wisdom, serving others, and putting the energy around you into higher order, greater harmony, and a more beautiful state. Let your prosperity be based on the amount of good you contribute to the world. It is not "higher" to be poor, for it often takes money to accomplish your life's work. Your spiritual growth will increase your ability to manifest abundance, and your ability to manifest will assist you in getting your spiritual work out to the world.

Money is a tremendous force. The way you earn your money, accumulate it, and spend it determines whether your money will be a force that creates good or doesn't create good for you and others. It is important to hold new thoughts about money that will help it be used as a force for good on the planet. Form follows thought; by holding new thoughts you can create new realities about money for yourself and others. Each of you can act as a powerful broadcasting station, sending out positive ideas about money and contributing to a higher vision of money on the planet.

Beliefs in scarcity help create your wars and the taking of more than is needed from the earth. If everyone could create the abundance that is his or her natural birthright, you would have fewer reasons for war or to harm the earth. Your new beliefs will draw to you ways to create abundance for everyone, ways you have not even conceived of yet that tap into sunlight and other unlimited resources. The universal supply is infinite, and it is within your technology and reach for every human being on the planet to live with enough food, warmth, clothing, and shelter. Until you believe that, you won't experience it, but you can start by believing that it is possible to have all your own needs met. There is no limit to what you may have!

Embrace fully your capacity to create, to think in unlimited ways, and to pursue everything that you have been wanting. Be flexible, open, and willing to let the new come to you. You can learn to honor and nurture yourself, and to allow yourself to have more than you ever thought possible. We invite you to play with us in the higher realms and claim the abundance you so richly deserve. This can be the most joyous, prosperous, and creative time of your life.

Creating Money

You Are the Source

Becoming Abundant

Discovering What You Want

Magnetizing What You Want

CHAPTER 1

You
*A*re the *S*ource

Get quiet, close your eyes, and think of something you
wanted that you got. Recall some of the feelings you had before
and after you received it—your positive thoughts about having
it, your inner knowing that you would have it, and your joy
when you received it. You manifest things naturally and automatically all the time, using your thoughts and feelings to
create what you want. Manifestation is a process of bringing
your ideas, concepts, visions, and dreams from your inner
world into your outer world where you can experience them
with your physical senses.

When you think of something you are fairly certain of
receiving, you have positive pictures; you can see yourself
having it and you don't worry about getting it. You want it,
intend to have it, and are motivated to do what is necessary
to bring it into your life. Begin to observe how you create
small, simple things. Start developing your manifesting skills
with things that are easy for you to create. As you gain confidence in your ability to create, you will be ready to manifest
in bigger, more unlimited ways. There is no limit to what you
can create. You live in a limitless world; anything is possible.

I *am the source of my abundance.*

You are the source of your abundance and money. Through working with your feelings, thoughts, and intentions, you can become a master at creating whatever you want. You are the source of your riches, not your job, your investments, your spouse, or your parents. By linking with the unlimited abundance of your soul or higher self, by opening your connection to the higher forces (sometimes called God, the All-That-Is, the Universal Mind, Christ, or Buddha), by expressing and radiating your higher qualities of inner peace, joy, love, well-being, and aliveness, you become the source of your abundance.

Having money and things is not as important as mastering the process of creating them. Once you master the process your ability to be prosperous will not be determined by the economy or outside conditions, for you will be able to create whatever you want when you want it. Learning to create abundance is a process of growth; it may require changing your thinking and expanding your beliefs about what you deserve to have. The process of getting each new thing—be it a car, a house, or a larger salary—will bring you growth, learning, and new skills. As you master the process, you will be able to use money and other things you create as tools for expanding your consciousness and helping you express yourself more fully.

Your thoughts have real substance, although your scientific instruments can't yet measure them. You might imagine your thoughts as "magnets." These "magnets" go out into the world and attract the substances that match them; they duplicate themselves in form. Everything around you was a thought in someone's mind before it existed in your reality. Cars, roads, homes, buildings, and cities all existed as thoughts before they became realities.

Your thoughts set up the model of what is to be created, and your emotions energize your thoughts and propel them from your inner world to your outer world. The stronger your emotions are, the more rapidly you create what you are thinking about. Your intent acts to direct your thoughts and emotions, maintaining a steady focus on what you want until you get it.

I *focus on what I love and thus draw it to me.*

Because your thoughts set up the model of what you draw to you, it is important to think about what you want rather than what you don't want. You will not get what you want by fearing or hating its opposite. For instance, having money does not come from disliking living in poverty. Whatever you focus on is what you get, for energy follows thought. The more you love having money and abundance, the more you picture it and thus draw it to you.

It is also important to think in positive ways. Positive emotions and thoughts draw what you want to you. Negative emotions do not bring what you want; they bring only what you don't want. Spend quiet, reflective time thinking positively about what you want. When you do not think in higher ways, dwelling on things such as problems, you repel abundance.

Don't feel bad about negative thoughts you have, for fearing or disliking your negative thoughts gives them more power. Respond to negative thoughts as you would to small children who don't know any better; simply smile and show them a better way to be. If you recognize a negative thought, simply place a positive thought alongside it. If, for instance, you catch yourself saying "I don't have enough money," simply say "I have an abundance of money."

M*y thoughts are loving and positive.*

Positive thoughts are far more powerful than negative thoughts. One positive thought can cancel out hundreds of negative ones. Your soul stops your lower and negative thoughts from becoming realities unless having them manifest will teach you something that will help you grow. You are loved and protected by your soul and the universe. As your thoughts become higher and more positive, your soul allows more and more of them to manifest. The more you evolve, the more power your thoughts have to create your reality, and the more responsibility you have to think in higher ways.

There are many wonderful tools you can use to learn to think more positively. For instance, you can put light—an image of physical light—into the pictures in your mind. You can practice making negative thoughts fade out or dissolve, and enlarging positive thoughts. Take a moment right now to think of something you want. Select one thought you have had about why you CAN'T have it. Now, imagine that thought fading out, or imagine that thought written on a blackboard that you are erasing, or imagine putting that thought in a balloon and letting it float away. Do whatever occurs to you to remove that thought from your reality.

Now, create a thought about why you CAN have it. See that thought written out; put white light around it. Imagine someone reading the thought to you in a beautiful voice. Create a mental image of receiving or having what you want. Make the image so real you can almost touch, smell, see, and feel it. Make the image bigger, so that you are standing in the image rather than just observing it. By making your negative thoughts fade out, you take away their power to create your reality. By making your positive thoughts more vivid and real, you increase their ability to create what you want.

There is great power in repeating the thought of something you want over and over. When you got something you wanted in the past you probably thought about it frequently. Repetition firmly implants the idea of what you want to create in your subconscious, and it goes about bringing you what you think about. You want the thought to be definite and unwavering. Affirmations are positive thoughts that are repeated over and over. As you repeat them, they go directly to your subconscious where they begin to manifest as your reality. Affirm what you want in present terms, such as, "I have unlimited abundance," and repeat your positive statements frequently.

Some of your negative thoughts may come from being around people whose fears and doubts amplify your own. For instance, you may feel fine about your finances, but after you talk to a friend who is struggling and fearful about money, you start worrying about your own financial future. If you notice this happening, realize that you have been influenced by someone else's thoughts, and remind yourself that you live in an abundant world and that all is perfect in your universe.

Large groups of people generate powerful thought-forms that may affect your thinking. For instance, at times some people are fearful about the economy; they think that a depression or recession is coming. If you are worried about the economy, you may be unconsciously tuning in to their thoughts and fears and responding to them as if they were your own. Wherever you are, there are some people who feel they are living in troubled economic times and others who feel that the times are the best they have ever been. You create your prosperity no matter what the economy is like. Your challenge is to keep your thoughts about your economic future positive and not be affected by what large groups of people are thinking or saying. Even during the worst economic times there are businesses and people who do quite well. You are the source of your abundance, and you can have a wonderful, positive, and abundant life regardless of the economy or other outside conditions.

My choices and possibilities are expanding every day.

Since your thoughts create your reality, you can create an even better life for yourself by learning to think in bigger and unlimited ways. Unlimited thinking increases creativity, expands your possibilities, draws opportunities to you, and allows you to have more. Unlimited thinking lets you experience in advance the feelings you will have when you have received the abundance you want, and these feelings are the vehicle that brings abundance to you. Use these visions to open your mind to greater possibilities.

Unlimited thinking helps you get in touch with the larger picture of your life and links you with the greater vision of your higher self. It helps you fulfill your potential. All great works start with a vision. Those of you who have children often engage in the process of unlimited thinking for them, weaving around them visions of who they might be and the great things they might accomplish. You help them recognize their ability to create whatever is best for them. When you are in love you recognize the potential that lies within the other person and help him or her create it. Unlimited thinking means having the same wonderful visions for yourself, recognizing and fulfilling your potential. Every time you think of the future you are creating a possible direction.

To unfold your potential you will want to imagine having your dreams come true, for your dreams and fantasies are showing you your potential. Your dreams are there for a reason; they are guiding you to your higher path here on earth. Enlarge your vision of what is possible for you to do.

Dare to dream and think big. If you are thinking of starting a business, don't compromise on what you think you can have or do. If you are thinking of serving one client a week, think of serving five. If you are thinking of starting your work in a year, think about what it would be like to start it in a month. Pretend that it is one year from today and you are reflecting back on all your accomplishments. What did you accomplish over the last year?

I *love and trust my imagination.*

To expand your thinking is to develop your imagination. Your imagination is greater in its scope than you might think. It is the closest link to your soul. It is not bound by your past programs, beliefs, and fears. Imagination was given to you so you could transcend your physical world. It gives you the ability to step outside of your personal limits and unleash your greatest potential. Your imagination can travel into any dimension or world. It can create unlimited future pathways for you and help you look at the possible outcomes of various choices.

Use your imagination and your ability to daydream and fantasize. Don't think "That's impossible; it can't be done." Think in possibilities. Rather than thinking of just one thing you could have that would satisfy you, think of many things. Instead of imagining only one desirable outcome, ask yourself, "What is the best possible outcome that can occur?" After you have imagined the best possible outcome, push yourself to imagine an even better one. Every time you find yourself imagining something, see if you can expand or fine-tune the picture. Think big! Ask for more than you think you can have. Expand your imagination, enlarge your pictures, and play with new ideas. See if you can go beyond the boundaries you have set for what you think you can have.

I *am an unlimited being.*
I can create anything I want.

When you begin practicing unlimited thinking, you may find that some of your earlier thoughts are still creating your reality. You may still meet the results of your past limited thinking while you are sending out your new unlimited thoughts. Don't be discouraged if you don't see results overnight. Gradually the old thought patterns will leave and you will experience the results of your new thinking.

On the earth plane you learn about manifesting in a linear, sequential way. You get to think about what you want, you get to rethink it, and you get to try it out. You can say "No, this isn't what I really wanted," or "Next time I think I'll ask for something different." You have the opportunity to play with all the things you create. The earth plane is a special place. It enables you to practice becoming clear on your thoughts before they are manifested all about you. Although you might complain that it takes longer for some things to appear than you want, most of you would be unhappy if you manifested all of the things you thought about instantaneously. By the time you get something, you have usually gone through a process of growth and gaining clarity about what you want.

Allow yourself to expand your ideas about what is possible and do not worry if you don't yet have the skills to create it. As you expand your thinking, your ability to manifest what you are dreaming about will develop as well. The more you expand the horizons of your imagination, opening new territories and going beyond what you think is possible, the more you open the doorway to unlimited abundance.

If you can't believe that something is possible, then you aren't going to have it. But if you can have the smallest thought that it might be possible, you are already on your way to creating it. You cannot create something if you cannot picture having it. Live out your dreams in your mind; picture or feel yourself getting what you want; hear the words you will say to others and they to you when your dreams come true. Make your imaginings so real that they feel possible to create rather than like wishful and distant fantasies.

Allow yourself to create a vision, to daydream and fantasize, and then focus each day on the simple, concrete steps you can take to reach your goal. There will always be practical steps you can take immediately to get there. Sometimes cleaning your house and putting all of your papers in order may be the next step to creating your vision of yourself as a teacher helping to organize a group of people.

I *picture abundance for myself and others.*

Picture yourself having everything you want—a satisfying job, money in the bank, a wonderful relationship. See how you would be a benefit to those around you. Imagine what it would be like if everyone you knew had money, and their lives were working. Challenge yourself to ask for even more, not just for yourself, but for all of mankind.

For instance, if you have been wanting a better job, picture that everyone who has been wanting one will get one also. If you want to serve in a larger way, such as drawing more students into your classes, imagine that everyone who is asking for a greater opportunity to serve through getting more students is also succeeding. This will teach you that there is true abundance in the universe for everyone, and help you connect your abundance with thoughts of abundance for everyone else. As you enlarge your thinking to include others, imagining abundance for everyone, you will open up even more ways for abundance to come to you.

Unlimited thinking is more than thinking big; it is thinking creatively. It is allowing yourself to imagine having all that you might have. Be open to pleasant surprises, for your higher self may bring you what you want in a bigger and better way than you thought possible. Trust that you will receive whatever is perfect for you to have.

The emotions behind your thoughts determine the speed at which you manifest. If you truly want something, it will come much more rapidly than if you are lukewarm about wanting it. Generate excitement about having what you want. Make it so real in your imagination that you can almost touch it, see it, or feel the feelings you will have when it comes to you. Think of it frequently and with intensity, and also be willing to detach and let it come in whatever way is best.

To manifest what you want, intend to create it. In other words, make up your mind that having what you want is important to you and that you are willing to put a certain amount of thought and energy into getting it. Your intent to have something directs your energy and focuses it on your goals. You create what you are picturing by concentrating on it with attention and awareness, and keeping it in the back of your mind even when you are involved in other activities.

When you hold a steady focus on having something, your intent to have it is clear and strong, and you create what you seek more rapidly. You are alert and able to take advantage of opportunities when they come. You draw things to you with ease and joy. Think of something you want right now. Do you intend to have it? Do you think about it even when you are doing other activities?

There may have been times when you really intended to have something, and you did anything necessary within your values and integrity to get it. You overcame obstacles. You knew in advance that you were going to get it; you thought about it positively, and you couldn't wait to have it. On the other hand, when you tried to create something you weren't sure you intended to have, you probably gave up as soon as an obstacle appeared to stand in your way. If you think what you want is too far away or hard to get, your intent is not clear.

When you have a clear intention to have something, you generate energy that is focused like a laser beam to go out and get what you want. If you intend to have something, you will.

My *dreams come true.*

EXERCISE:

Learning to Relax, Focus, and Visualize

Visualizing is using your imagination to picture what you want in advance of getting it. The more real you can make your expanded, unlimited thoughts, the more easily you can create them. Your imagination is your most powerful energy-creating tool. When using your imagination there are no rules other than being as inventive as you can. You use your ability to visualize all the time. You make pictures in your mind prior to creating anything. As you pretend that you already have something, you begin to harmonize with it and bring the feeling of having it into your present reality. This feeling begins to draw it to you.

Do not worry if you can't actually picture what you are thinking about, for not all people see a mental image when they imagine something. Some people feel it or have a sense of it and some people simply think about it. Others make mental pictures of varying degrees of clarity and color. It is not necessary to see mental pictures clearly in order to create something you want. Most people find that visualizing gets easier as they practice.

Focusing is holding a thought or picture steadily in your mind without thinking of other things. Concentrating on what you want by focusing steadily on it for several minutes at a time increases the speed with which you draw things to you. The exercise that follows will assist you in relaxing, focusing, and visualizing. It is basic preparation for working with energy and magnetizing in Chapter 4.

Preparation:

Pick a time when you will be undisturbed for at least fifteen minutes. Create an enjoyable, soothing environment around you. You may want to play some calming, soothing music. Have a favorite small object nearby, something you can hold in your hands, such as a piece of jewelry or a crystal.

Steps:

1. Find a comfortable sitting position, either in a chair or on the floor, which you can easily hold for ten or fifteen minutes. If possible, your spine should be straight to allow a good energy flow through your body. Close your eyes and begin breathing calmly and slowly, taking about twenty slow, rhythmic, connected breaths into your upper chest.

2. Relax your body. Feel yourself growing serene, calm, and tranquil. In your imagination, travel through your body, relaxing each part. Mentally relax your feet, legs, thighs, stomach, chest, arms, hands, shoulders, neck, head, and face. Let your jaw be slightly loose, and relax the muscles around your eyes. Feel yourself growing even calmer. Think of a time when you felt great inner peace, and bring that feeling into your body now.

3. With your eyes closed, think of a room in your house. How do you think of it? Do you see it as if you were looking at a movie screen, or do you feel you are standing in the room and looking at it through your eyes as if you were there? Do you sense the room around you? Is it in color? Can you recreate the arrangement of the furniture? Can you imagine yourself walking around the room? Recall an image or a feeling of the room as vividly as possible for a minute or so, then let it fade.

4. Open your eyes. Pick up the object you chose earlier. Look at it closely, noticing the color, shape, weight, feel, texture, and as many other details as you can. After a few minutes put the object down, put your hands in the same position they were in when you were holding the object, and close your eyes. Now, recreate the image of the object in your mind in as much detail as possible. With your eyes closed, can you picture its color, shape, weight, texture, and how it felt in your hand?

5. Now think of a small object you want to have that you don't yet have. For this exercise, use something you have

seen before. With your eyes closed, picture the object as completely as you can. How would it feel? What color and shape would it have?

6. Now practice expanding your imagination by taking the object you just visualized and imagining an even better one. How does it feel when you picture having something that is even better than you thought you could have? Of course, if the object you visualized originally is just what you want, you don't need to ask for something better. It is good, however, to practice expanding your imagination.

7. Think of this object you want to bring into your life. Focus your mind. For one or two minutes, think of that thing to the exclusion of anything else. If any thoughts come up that you do not want, simply imagine putting them in a bubble and letting them float away.

8. When you feel calm and relaxed and ready to return, bring your attention slowly back into the room. Savor and enjoy your state of calmness and peace. View the world around you from this brighter, clearer perspective.

Evaluation:

If you feel calmer, more relaxed, or balanced, you have achieved the state of consciousness necessary to magnetize. The calmer and more focused you are and the higher your thoughts, the better your results will be when you magnetize what you want in Chapter 4. If you don't feel relaxed and centered, work with this or other meditations until you do.

Notice how you visualize things. Do you sense them or see them? Are they in color? How clear are they? Keep practicing until you can experience an inner picture or sense of what you want. If you are satisfied with your ability to visualize and you were able to focus on what you wanted for several minutes, move on to the next chapter. If you weren't able to focus on what you wanted for several minutes, play with focusing several more times while you read the next chapter.

CHAPTER 2

Becoming Abundant

Whether you are consciously aware of it or not, deep inside you are seeking growth and aliveness, wanting to manifest your potential and be all you can be. Most people are seeking a life filled with joy, love, a feeling of security, creative self-expression, enjoyable and meaningful activities, and self-esteem. The more of these aspects you have in your life the more fulfilled you will feel and the more you will be realizing your full potential. An important part of manifesting is learning to create only those things that fulfill your deepest needs and serve as tools to help you grow and have the best life possible.

The desire to create something new, whether it is a pair of shoes, a new house, or a large sum of money, comes because you are ready to grow and achieve more of your potential. Most people think that having money will fill a need, allowing them to experience a feeling, quality, or situation they don't now have. Some people think a large sum of money will give them feelings of aliveness, well-being, self-esteem, inner peace, love, power, or security. They think with money they will be free from worry and will be able to relax and play, or not do activities they don't want to do.

Money and objects by themselves will not automatically fill your needs or give you the feelings you want. If you think that having more money will give you inner peace, allowing the quality of inner peace into your life is your key to becoming magnetic to more money. Whatever you think having more money will give you—aliveness, peace, self-esteem—is the quality you need to develop to become more magnetic to money and abundance. View money and things *not* as something you create to fill a lack, but as tools to help you more fully express yourself and realize your potential.

One man wanted to create a million dollars. He didn't care how he did it; to him a million dollars was just money he thought would magically make his life perfect. In truth, although he wasn't aware of it, he wanted the money to feel more alive. Because he wasn't aware of why he wanted the money he didn't ask, "What can I do that would make me feel more alive?" Instead he said to himself, "I will work harder even though I don't enjoy my work. I will spend even less time doing things I love so I can spend more hours working for the money I need. I will forgo pleasure right now. I will have everything after I get the money." He found that he disliked going to work even more. Because he didn't like his job he didn't give it his best effort, and he was passed up for promotions.

He heard about many get-rich-quick schemes, and invested all his extra money in several of them, even borrowing on some of his credit cards to do so. Unfortunately they didn't turn out well, and he lost a lot of money. Twenty years later he was still working at the same job, complaining about not being appreciated at work, and looking for the next get-rich-quick "scheme" that would be his magical key to wealth and the good life. He planned to do all the things he had always wanted to do when the money came. Yet, because he did not do the things that helped him feel alive, he never did get the money he sought.

I *live in an abundant universe.*
I always have everything I need.

Stop for a moment and ask yourself what you think having more money will give you that you don't now have. What deeper needs or desires would be satisfied if you had a large sum of money? Would you have more security, freedom from worry, a simpler life? Would you be able to stop doing activities you don't want to do, have no problems, or the freedom to do what you want with your life? What higher qualities or feelings do you think you would have more of— inner peace, love, self-esteem, well-being, happiness? If it isn't a large sum of money you want but an object or item that you don't yet have, what needs will this item satisfy in your life? If there isn't anything material that you want, what higher quality or feeling would you like to experience more frequently?

You can start satisfying those needs right now. You can have a joyful, fulfilling life and realize your greater potential without the material things you want to create. The essence of anything that will serve your higher good is within your reach. The universe doesn't say you can have what is good for you only after you make a million dollars. The universe says that whatever is for your higher good you can have right now, today. Ask yourself what you want money to give you and then think of ways you could have the essence of those things right now.

For instance, some people think that having money will make their lives simpler. You can have a simpler life right now by developing and expressing the qualities that will allow you to do so, such as inner peace, well-being, or inner silence. Money will not give you a simpler life. In fact, if you do not learn to bring those qualities into your life that make your life simpler, money may make your life more complex rather than simplify it. If you have been wanting a simpler life, what could you do right now to begin to simplify your life?

Some people hope that when they have money they will be able to stop doing the things they don't enjoy. To begin to let go of doing things you don't enjoy, learn to honor and respect yourself more. You can begin by learning how to stop doing the small things you don't enjoy right now; as you do you gain more honor and respect for yourself and will build up to doing *only* things you enjoy. Some people are motivated to make money because they think that having it will take away their problems and lessons. You cannot live on earth and avoid lessons; but you can learn them easily and with joy rather than struggle. Developing the qualities of inner wisdom and peace will help you see your problems as opportunities for growth, which will help you deal with them more easily than having money ever will.

You may want a large sum of money in order to feel secure. Security does not come from accumulating wealth. Some people have created multi-million-dollar empires and still do not feel secure. In fact, if they do not learn to feel secure, more money may amplify their feelings of insecurity or intensify their fears. For you, feeling secure might come from developing qualities such as courage and trusting your inner guidance. If you have a feeling of security within, you will be able to create a life that reflects that feeling. If you want more security in your life, stop for a moment, get quiet, and ask yourself what quality you could develop that would help you feel more secure.

Some people want money because they think it will make them feel more powerful. We are not referring to ego power, the kind that manipulates or controls others, but true power, which comes from reaching upward, gaining inner peace, manifesting your potential, and operating from the light of your soul rather than from your personality. What qualities, if you experienced them more often, would assist you in experiencing more personal power? Find ways to express these qualities and do these activities more often.

I *radiate self-esteem, inner peace, love,*
well-being, and happiness.

As you express the higher qualities you think more money will give you, radiating those qualities outward with your words, actions, and being, you will become magnetic to money and objects that are physical expressions of your new level of consciousness. Developing any higher quality—be it love, inner peace, well-being, happiness, courage, personal power, or self-respect—will change your vibration and make you magnetic to whatever matches your new vibration. You will become magnetic not only to more money, but to all the forms that will help you express your new level of growth. You will draw to you the things you know you want, as well as having things come to you before you are aware you need them. You will attract things that are better than what you ask for and everything around you will fit who you are.

One man's goal for fifteen years was to create a million dollars, retire, and take life easy. One day he realized that he was hardly any closer to having this sum than he had been years earlier. He had tried in every way he knew to get rich. He had made various investments with mixed results, had worked as hard as he could at his job, and had saved a small sum for his retirement. He took the time to think about what a million dollars would give him, and decided it would allow him time to relax and give him freedom to do some of the activities he loved. He decided to start finding time for relaxation and the activities he loved without having the money first, since it appeared that if he waited for the money he might never live the life he wanted.

After trying several approaches to relaxing, he realized that he needed to develop the quality of self-respect, for every time he tried to take time to relax or do the activities he loved other obligations and duties would stop him. He looked at what self-respect meant to him, and decided it meant giving himself permission to spend quiet time alone and to pursue some hobbies that gave him joy. He started playing a musical instrument he had loved playing earlier in his life. As he spent more time alone, many wonderful melodies and lyrics went through his mind and he recorded them. As he pursued his music, he found his creativity opening up in other areas of his life. His self-respect began to increase. He got a promotion at work and a job offer for much more pay, which he took. Eventually he sold the music he composed to several movie companies, and he was on his way to greater wealth than he had ever known. By developing self-respect he created not only the money he wanted, but many other wonderful things as well—a job he loved, a life that was fulfilling and satisfying, and an opportunity to realize his greater potential and skills.

I *create money and abundance through joy, aliveness, and self-love.*

If you are in touch with the needs you want money to fulfill and the higher qualities you hope it will bring you, and you work on developing those qualities, the money and objects you attract will bring you joy and self-fulfillment. If you don't know what deeper needs and higher qualities you want to express by having something, you may or may not be satisfied with it when you receive it, even though you are able to attract it. You may be making more money right now than at another time of your life, and yet not feel any more abundant or rich than you did at a lower income. If your inner needs are not satisfied, no amount of money will feel like enough.

You can create money through greed, not honoring others, or for other reasons that do not help you live a satisfying life. You do not have to grow and start realizing your potential to attract large sums of money. But the way you create money and objects determines the lessons and growth you experience. If you create money through greed, for instance, it may be sought after by others or you may lose it quickly. You may bring to yourself many lessons about greed, including worry and fear. The money you attract may amplify the problems you want it to solve.

Everything I do brings me aliveness and growth.

Once you have identified the deeper needs you think money will fulfill and the higher qualities you want to experience more frequently, you can start fulfilling those needs and expressing those qualities in many ways. One way is to make a mental list of all the activities that help you experience a desired feeling, and resolve to do them more often. For instance, if you want more aliveness, you may decide that the activities that help you feel more alive are quality times with friends and family, walks in the park, good movies, and spending time on a creative hobby. Once you identify the activities that make you feel alive, do them more often. If feeling more alive is what you think money will give you, doing those things that make you feel more alive is what will make you magnetic to money and abundance.

If you don't know what activities help you feel alive or peaceful or whatever feeling you want more of, you can start by remembering the times you experienced those feelings in the past. What activities were you doing? If you don't think you have experienced much aliveness in the past, look at your life right now and ask what situations or activities, even the smallest ones, bring you more aliveness. Begin to focus on the times you do feel alive; observe what you are doing and do those activities more frequently. As you build on those, you will come up with even more ways to feel alive. Begin by doing what you know how to do right now. Do not wait to take action until your skills are more advanced, for your ability to manifest is developed step by step. Don't try to have everything all at once. Take one small step at a time and your success will build on itself. You will feel alive (or whatever quality you want to feel) more and more frequently, until that feeling is part of who you have become.

One woman decided that the quality she wanted was a feeling of aliveness, and she realized that it came through taking classes at the local college, spending an hour several times a week reading a book, and treating herself to frequent long, warm soaks in the bathtub. A man wanted more inner peace, and he realized that what gave it to him was frequent exercise, an occasional weekend spent fishing, and time to build a small workshop for himself where he could put his tools and build things.

As you experience more inner peace, joy, aliveness, or any of your higher qualities, you move to the next level of your personal evolution. You become more fulfilled, happy with yourself, and able to create a life filled with creative self-expression, enjoyable and meaningful activities, and feelings of self-love, self-worth, and self-esteem. As you express more and more of whatever higher quality you think more money will give you, you become magnetic not only to more money but also to abundance in every area of your life. You are a magnificent and powerful being. Believe that you deserve to have the best life you can imagine!

The process of getting there is the quality of being there.

EXERCISE:

Expressing a Higher Quality

You can use this exercise to learn to express a higher quality more often by visualizing having and being that quality.

Preparation:

Find a time and place where you can relax and think without interruption. Relax as in the *Learning to Relax* exercise on page 14.

Steps:

1. Close your eyes and think of a higher quality you would like to have more of in your life such as courage, peace, happiness, well-being, or love. Preferably, choose a quality you think having more money will give you. As you think of this quality, imagine you are feeling it. What does it feel like? Can you bring the feeling into your body? Notice any changes in your posture or breathing as you feel it in your body.

2. Picture a future situation in which you are expressing or experiencing this feeling. Pick one scene in your mind—a future imaginary event that represents how you might experience that quality. For instance, if you want more inner peace in your life, you might think of a common situation you experience often and see yourself experiencing inner peace the next time it happens. Keep the picture simple. Repeat it in your mind over and over. Feel the feelings you want to have in this situation as if you do have them.

3. Notice how you are picturing this scene. Do you picture who is present, the clothes you are wearing, or what setting you are in? Fill out the picture in your mind with as many details as you can imagine.

4. Observe your picture of the scene again. Is it bright or dim? Make the picture brighter and notice your feelings of this higher quality as you do.

5. Are you seeing this as a picture in front of you, as if you are looking at a movie screen, or are you in the picture? Is the picture small or large? Is it in front of you or far away? Make the picture so real that you are standing inside of it.

6. If someone is talking to you, make his or her voice beautiful, pleasing, and rich. Add pleasing, beautiful sounds to your picture—perhaps sounds of nature, the ocean, or beautiful music in the background.

7. Make the setting even more beautiful and pleasant. In your mind make the colors more intense. Feel the objects in the scene and imagine the smells. Let the picture be 360 degrees wide, all around you, above you, and a part of you. Make the feeling of inner peace or whatever quality you want even more real. If your thoughts wander, bring them back to your scene and the quality you want.

8. The more vividly you can picture your scene or feel the quality, the better. See yourself enjoying having that feeling or quality. Make the picture so real you can almost touch, hear, and see it. Bring in the full play of your emotions.

9. Slowly let the scene fade. Enjoy your feelings as long as you like, then open your eyes. Take a deep breath and bring your full attention back to your present reality.

Evaluation:

The more you can put yourself in the picture, rather than just seeing it as something outside of you (as if you are watching a movie), the more easily and rapidly you will create the feeling of the quality you want. The more real you can make your imaginary scene and the feelings of this quality, the more frequently you will experience having this quality in your life. If you can't picture a scene, you can draw a quality to you by simply thinking of that quality as often as you can remember. Imagine you are feeling it. Bring the feeling into your body and make it as real as possible.

CHAPTER 3

Discovering
What You Want

You may have many ideas about specific objects, sums of money, and other things that you want to create. Some of these things you want can help you express your higher qualities more fully, and some may not. You may have experienced this when you got something you thought you wanted and it didn't bring you the satisfaction you thought it would. You can learn to attract only those things that are the best tools for expressing your higher qualities and fulfilling your deeper needs, and be satisfied with everything you create.

In the next chapter, *Magnetizing What You Want*, you will learn how to work with your energy and magnetism to draw what you want to you. Before you magnetize, you will want clarity about what you want. You will want to know the essence something will give you, the needs it will fulfill, and the higher qualities you can express more fully to fulfill those needs. In this chapter you will learn how to get clear about the essence of what you want, as well as its specific form if you know it. Then, when you magnetize what you want and it comes to you, it will be in a form that truly satisfies you and brings you joy. As a result you will draw things to you that are even better than what you imagine.

You can effectively draw things to you whether or not you know the specific form, amount, or appearance of the items you want. You do need to know their essence, however. The essence of something is the function you want this item to perform, the purposes you will use it for, or what you think it will give you. Many things other than what you picture might give you the essence of what you want, so be open to letting what you want come in whatever way, size, shape, or form is most appropriate.

I *know the essence of what I want and I get it.*

By knowing the essence of what you want you make it possible to get it in many ways. For instance, if the essence of what you want from a new car is more reliable transportation, you might be able to find many ways to create that besides buying a new car. If you don't know the essence of what you want, you may buy a new car that is just as unreliable as the one you have.

One woman wanted a new car because the car she had was unreliable and she was concerned about driving places at night. She didn't dislike her car or want to spend money on a new one, but she thought the only way to have a reliable car was to get a new one. She got quiet and visualized a car, and magnetized its essence—reliability—to her. Coincidentally, her old car stopped having problems! She got a new car several years later, and it was very reliable also. The essence of her request came to her quickly, although not in the way she imagined.

You may want a new coat. Getting specific about the features you want in a coat will lead you to the essence of what the coat will give you. You may decide that it must be very warm, have a pleasing appearance, and be durable. As you become clear about the essence of what you want, you will realize that many coats could fulfill your needs. You may also discover that in addition to coats, other forms such as sweaters or heavy shirts might work as well. By becoming clear on the essence you want, you increase the range of possible forms and ways in which these forms can come to you. If you don't know the essence of what you want, you might buy a coat and find out later that it isn't warm enough in snow, or dry enough in rain, or cannot take the heavy wear you subject it to.

You may not know exactly what features will best suit your requirements. You may want a new home but not know where it will be or how many rooms it will have. In this case, you can get specific about what functions it will fill in your life and how you will use it. You might ask for a house that has morning sun and lots of light, is near trees, has room for a hobby area, offers privacy from neighbors, has an open feeling, and so on. These features are the essence of the house you want.

E*verything I create fulfills me.*

If you focus on appearance or picture your new home in great detail but are not clear on the functions you want your house to fulfill, you might get the specific appearance you want and find that the house doesn't serve your needs. If you buy a particular house just because you like the way it looks without knowing what you want to do in the house (such as entertain friends, store your outdoor equipment, or set up an office), the house might disappoint you. It might have too little space for entertaining, inadequate storage, and too few rooms. While it is good to picture a very specific house if you can, even down to the color of the walls, you also want to know why you want those particular features. Once you know the essence of what you want, the objects you attract will give you what you hope they will.

Even if you know the form of what you want, you still want to know the essence. To discover the essence, get as specific as you can. For instance, if you want a new television, think about the color, features, and options that you want; then ask, "Why do I want this feature instead of that one?" As you get more and more specific, you will discover the essence of what you want. If you have ever designed or built something, you may have discovered that you needed to think ahead to all the uses and functions you would want it to have in order for it to serve your purposes.

The things I create are even better than I imagine them to be.

If you ask for something indefinite, such as to be rich or happy, ask yourself, "How would I know if I were happy? How much money would I have in the bank to consider myself rich? How much monthly income? How much extra money to spend on certain items I want?" When you ask for extra money but you don't say how much, you may get an extra dollar rather than the larger but unstated amount you were thinking of. Ask for the specific amount of money you want; magnetize that sum or even more. Also picture the essence of what that money will give you and the higher qualities you want it to help you express.

When you magnetize something specific, ask, "What essence or functions do I want from this? What are all the ways I will use it? Is this the only acceptable form or way it can come? Am I being open to having the best thing come? Are there other forms that will fulfill the same functions in even better ways? Can I have the essence of what I want right now without waiting to buy this specific thing or have this sum of money?" When you magnetize, you can either picture the specific object you want and the functions and requirements you want it to fill, or picture the requirements you want it to fill and let it come in whatever is the best form. Either way will work.

Once you are clear about the essence of what you want, learn to recognize it when it comes. One woman wanted a new apartment and got very specific about the form. She wanted a place with a balcony, lots of sunlight, and a park nearby. She was also clear about what having these specific things would give her. The balcony would allow her to have a garden in which to grow vegetables, and the location would allow her to be outdoors with trees and fresh air. She worked with energy to draw to her both the apartment and the essence it would give her. Shortly thereafter, she met a new friend who was in the produce business, and he brought her many wonderful fresh vegetables. He loved the outdoors, and they spent many weekends hiking and camping in beautiful places. One day she realized that she already had the essence of what she wanted from a new apartment, and it had come in an even better way than she had imagined. If there is something you want but do not yet have, explore the essence of your request. Your soul brings you the essence of what you desire, although it may not be in the form you expect. The essence you want may have already come to you, and all you need do is recognize it.

To magnetize successfully, focus on creating what you want, not on getting rid of something you don't want. Many people do not know what they want, yet they are very clear on what they don't want. If you don't know what you want, you can start by looking at the circumstances in your life you don't like, and ask for an opposite circumstance to appear. For fun, ask your friends what would make them happy or what they want in their lives. You will be surprised at how many people will start by describing the conditions they don't want rather than the ones they want. For every condition you don't want, describe as clearly as you can what you would replace that condition with. State what you want in the present tense as an affirmation. Instead of saying "I don't want to struggle to pay my bills," you could say, "I pay my bills easily each month."

Another important aspect of magnetizing is to be sure that what you are asking for is something you can imagine having. If you want a million dollars, can you really imagine having it? A million dollars might not seem real to you, particularly if you have trouble imagining yourself paying your rent easily and on time each month. Your belief that it is possible may not be strong enough to draw this sum of money to you within a time frame that would give you an experience of success with your magnetizing.

It is best to start by asking for those things you can imagine yourself having. When you start with items that you believe are possible to create, you get to experience the successful results of your magnetism and energy work, which strengthens your belief in your ability to create what you want.

Each success builds on the one before. Your subconscious builds a stronger and stronger belief in your ability to manifest, and with that confidence it gains the ability to create more and more abundance for you. As you experience success, you develop a belief and an inner knowing that it is possible to create even those things that felt impossible when you started. It is that inner feeling—knowing that it is possible and even probable that you will have what you want—that is most important when you get ready to draw objects into your life.

Magnetize things you truly want, are prepared to have, and are excited about having. If, after thinking that you want something, you realize that you aren't truly prepared to go after it and make it your primary focus, it is better to let go of wanting it and put your energy into getting something else that is truly meaningful to you. If you aren't truly motivated and clear on your intent to have something, you may not draw it to you.

Magnetize what you truly want, not something that is a compromise. Acquiring objects that are compromises is rarely exciting enough to stimulate you to do what is necessary to get them. If you do not feel you can create what you want, it is better not to ask for something in its place that doesn't really excite or motivate you.

Many of you have a mental list of things you want that you don't yet have. Every time you refer to this list you think of all your unfulfilled wants and tell yourself that you aren't successful in creating what you want. Make a list of everything you have been thinking you want, and do some soul-searching. Do you really want these things? Are they old pictures of what you think you should want? Take all the unimportant things off your mental list, until you are left with only a few really important things that you want to create.

You are motivated to create the things you love, the things that bring you delight and not just relief. Many of you say to yourselves, "I should create money to pay off my debts, get my car fixed, or get this or that." "Shoulds" don't give you enough emotional energy to create abundance, and do not come from your higher self. Thinking you "should" pay off your debts is not enough motivation for most people, unless there is also some joy in doing so, such as a feeling of well-being and satisfaction in watching the debts disappear. It is better to acknowledge that you don't really want some of the things you have on your list, so you can focus instead on getting what you really do want.

My energy is focused and directed toward my goals.

Once you have made the decision that your goal is worth getting and putting energy into, make it a priority. You may not have to commit much energy, but be willing to do so if necessary. Pick the one or two most important things you could create in your life and focus on them. Ask yourself, "What is the single most important thing I could create in my life right now?" Then begin to create it. You can have whatever you believe you can have, and you can begin to have the essence of anything you want right now.

Be aware that once you start creating with energy and magnetism you are going to get what you ask for, usually more easily than you expect. Most things will come through your normal channels. If you usually buy things, that will probably be how you get the objects you magnetize. Don't invalidate your energy work because things come easily and naturally! You may be tempted to say, "This came so easily, it would have come anyway without my energy work and magnetism." Your skill in magnetizing will evolve and you will discover new techniques, so getting what you want will get easier and easier. After a while it may seem as if you didn't really do anything. Congratulate yourself when something you have been wanting comes into your life and recognize that you have succeeded in drawing it to you. Be willing to view everything that comes as an indication that your magnetism is working. Acknowledging each success makes it even easier to create the next thing you want.

DISCOVERING WHAT YOU WANT
PLAYSHEET

To bring together many of the things you have learned so far, think of something you want to create in your life, something that is a reach for you right now.

1 | Write down as specifically as you can what it is you want to create.

2 | Can you ask for something that is even better?

3 | What level of intention would it take to get it? (How much time, energy, commitment?)

4 | What quality do you hope having this object, sum of money, or thing will help you express? (Peace of mind, aliveness, freedom, love?)

5 | List several ways you can experience this quality right now.

6 | What are the essences that you expect this object or thing to give you? For instance, a new house may represent the desire for more space, sunlight, privacy, or a quieter environment.

7 | Are there alternative ways you might have these essences? What other things would provide the essence of what you want?

Gaining clarity about what you want is powerful in bringing something into your life in a way that will truly fulfill and satisfy you. Clarity makes the magnetism you will learn in the next chapter more effective. You will want to magnetize the essence something will give you, the thing itself, and the qualities you are seeking in having it.

CHAPTER 4

Magnetizing What You Want

Drawing the objects, forms, money, and people you want into your life is easier when you work with energy and magnetism before you take action. Creating with energy is done by getting quiet and relaxed, and then bringing images, symbols, and pictures of what you want into your mind. Magnetizing what you want requires generating a magnetic force to draw things to you.

You work with energy and magnetism all the time, though usually not consciously. You can learn to consciously work with energy and magnetism to amplify the power of your thoughts and create what you are picturing. A few moments of energy work, combined with magnetism and done with a sense of clarity about what you want, can create greater results than hours of hard work.

You are sending out an energy broadcast all the time. This broadcast may be attracting or repelling things you want. You can learn to increase your skill at magnetizing and become even more attractive to what you want. You start magnetizing what you want by working with your energy; learn to relax, focus, visualize, and use your imagination.

Magnetizing involves generating a magnetic field. The image of a "magnetic coil" is used to help you visualize and "feel" this magnetism. You can magnetize money, small or large objects, and indefinite things such as qualities and essence. You can also draw people to you who you will have a working relationship with, such as employers, employees, publishers, mechanics, and so on. You cannot use magnetism to change another person or force something to happen that is not in the best interests of both parties, for magnetism works only to draw those things to you that are in the best interests of all concerned.

Creativity, inventiveness, playfulness, and spontaneous imagination are your best tools when creating with energy. Every time you do the following magnetism exercises, you will notice that you have different thoughts, feelings, and ideas. Manifestation is a dynamic state; it is always changing. The intensity of your magnetism and your pictures may not be the same from one time to the next. Use and expand your imagination and play with whatever images and feelings come up. The feeling of magnetism is more important than any of the individual steps. Once you experience this feeling, recreate it with any visualization or picture that works for you.

I *am increasingly magnetic to money, prosperity, and abundance.*

There are some basic principles to becoming more magnetic to what you want. First, it is best if you know how what you are asking for will be a tool for whatever higher quality you want to express more frequently in your life. As you magnetize something, think of the quality you want to radiate. Second, it is helpful to magnetize the essence or features of what you want as well as the specific form. You can magnetize a symbol of what you want if you don't know its actual form. Symbols are very powerful because they bypass all your thoughts and beliefs about what you think is possible for you to have. Third, ask for what you want or even more. Fourth, love and intend to have what you are asking for. You will want to think positively of what you want, for high, positive thoughts are more magnetic than worry, fear, and tension. Fifth, believe that what you are asking for is possible to have. Sixth, it is important not to "need" what you are calling to you but rather to have a certain detachment about it. Let it be all right if it doesn't come, or if it comes in a different form than what you expect. After you have asked for something, surrender to whatever comes as being appropriate.

The easiest things to magnetize are small objects that are similar to other items you have already created, perhaps even in the same price range. It is good to start with something that you feel you can succeed in creating. Creating it will give you feedback and confidence in your developing magnetizing skill. As you practice on these smaller objects, see if you can fine-tune your ability to get exactly what you want or something even better than you are picturing. Play with how quickly and easily you can attract it. As your skill increases you can magnetize things that are larger, more expensive, or more challenging for you to believe you might have.

When you magnetize something there will be a point at which you suddenly feel it coming to you. It may feel as if there is a "click," or the feeling of building energy will begin to lessen. When you feel this, it is a signal that your magnetizing is complete, and you can stop magnetizing. If there has been no click, if you don't feel closer to having it, magnetize again until you feel an inner sense that the energy has shifted.

You have the ability to know when your magnetism is working. This inner knowing is developed over time, through observation and awareness of the process and through the feedback of the results you produce. As you practice, sometimes you will want to magnetize several times, and other times once will be enough.

Most of you use too much energy and power to create small results. You can learn how to put out a small amount of energy and create big results. There is a proper amount of energy for creating whatever you want. For instance, if you want to attract your next meal, you do not usually need to spend the entire day thinking about it and working at drawing it to you. Some of you use far too much of your vital force to attract something that is as simple to create as a meal. Learn to sense how much energy it will take to get what you want, then put out just that amount and no more.

I create what I want with energy.
Good things come to me easily.

If you are exerting too much energy it will feel like a strain. If you must constantly remind yourself to think about something you want and work on it, if magnetizing feels like a struggle and you are putting out a tremendous amount of energy for just a little or no result, you are putting out too much magnetic intensity. If you have to apply too much power, you are probably going against the current of your higher path. If when you think of something you can almost feel it coming, you are using the right amount of energy. If you use too small an amount it will not come to you at all or it may take a long time to come. You can know if you are exerting too small an amount of energy because what you want will seem far away; it will seem like a wish more than a certainty.

Before you attract something that has much larger energy than what you have now, learn to harmonize with its energy. For instance, if you want a sum of money that is much larger than what you have, you will want to be ready for it, know in advance how you are going to store it, what you will use it for, and how it will help your life. You will want to imagine how you will feel when you have it and resolve any concerns you may have about receiving it.

Before you magnetize anything that is much larger than what you have now, play with "wearing" the energy of what you will draw to you. Imagine that you already have it and look at how your life is different because of it. You can learn to harmonize and become familiar with things before you have them; as you do you will become more magnetic to having them.

One way to harmonize with something that is much larger than you have now is to expand what you have asked for. If you want a sum of money that is much larger than what you have, try "wearing" an even larger sum. Continue trying out increasingly larger sums of money. You will notice that as the amount increases, the way you feel and think changes. Some amounts may feel comfortable, but higher sums may feel slightly uncomfortable. As you "wear" larger sums, you may find that a smaller sum that initially felt uncomfortable becomes more comfortable. Only magnetize what feels comfortable and possible to have.

The more you feel comfortable with money or anything at an energy level before you magnetize it, the more easily it will come to you. Observe closely how your thoughts about yourself might change, how your feelings and your lifestyle would be different. Doing this should draw out any hidden fears, such as, "Having this might mean too much responsibility, or I'll have to worry more about taxes and accountants, people will want my money," and so on. As you deal with these doubts or worries, you make it possible to become more magnetic to what you want.

When you first work with these exercises the results may be less consistent and the timing less controllable than you would like. Eventually the steps will become automatic, and the amount of work you do to magnetize what you want will decrease each time. Do these exercises only as long as you find them enjoyable and interesting. Magnetize what you want as frequently as you like, for a few minutes or half an hour. After you master one level of magnetism, you might still need to work a bit more to produce results at your next level and attract things that are hard for you to accept as possible in your life.

Once you master creating a particular type of thing, all you will usually need to do in the future is think of it for it to manifest readily. If you are able to manifest something easily and then the flow stops or begins to lessen, or attracting it requires too much work, it may be time to examine more carefully the path you are on. Pay close attention to any whispers of new directions that are emerging.

Sanaya and Duane: You can do these exercises by yourself, with a partner, or with a group of people. If you are doing them alone, you may want to tape record the instructions and play them back, as they will lead you step by step into the process of magnetism. If you have a partner, you may want your partner to read the instructions to you. For your convenience, we have prepared an audio cassette tape of the General Magnetizing process you can use. (Refer to *Additional Resources* in back of book for information.) If you are with a group, you may want one person to read the instruction to the entire group. If you skipped the exercise on relaxing in Chapter 1, be sure that you are relaxed, focused, and feeling peaceful when you use the magnetism exercises that follow. You may want to keep a record of what you are asking for, and be willing to recognize it when it comes.

EXERCISE:

General Magnetizing

You can use this exercise to learn how to create something you want with energy and magnetism. This can be a small or large object, a sum of money, or the essence of what you want.

Preparation:

Pick something you want. It is important that you believe it is possible to have, think positively about it, and intend to have it. Be as specific as you can about the higher quality it will give you, and imagine this higher quality as you magnetize. You will also want to magnetize the essence it will give you and the specific form or amount of money if you know it. Expand your imagination and see if you can ask for even more. If you do not know the form, you can magnetize a symbol that represents it. Take a moment now to think of what you want. You may want to use the playsheet *Discovering What You Want* in Chapter 3 on page 35 to assist you in getting as clear as possible about what you want.

Find a time and place where you can relax and think without interruption for a few minutes. Relax and prepare yourself in the same way as in the *Learning to Relax* exercise on page 14. Remember that what is important is the feeling of magnetism. An image of a coil is used because it has been most effective in helping people obtain the "feeling" of magnetism. Once you have achieved this feeling-state, use whatever picture or thought helps you to recreate this feeling in the future. This exercise uses your imagination; there are no "right" or "wrong" ways to do it. The best results come from playing with the sensations and pictures, and being creative and inventive as you magnetize.

Steps:

1. Think of what you have chosen to magnetize. Get as specific as you can about the details of the item if you know

them, and all the functions and features—the essences—that you want.

2. Visualize or sense what you want, making the picture as real as possible. Create a scene in which you imagine yourself receiving it, living out the good feelings you will have as you get it. Enhance your visualization, as in the *Learning to Relax* exercise on page 14. If you cannot visualize what you want, imagine as vividly as possible the feeling that having it will bring you. Or, pick a symbol that represents this item or thing, and work with the symbol. Use this same picture or symbol every time you magnetize or think about the thing you have chosen.

3. Imagine that you have a power source within you that generates energy. Then picture a coil, like a loop, that goes around and around. This coil begins in the area near your solar plexus inside your body and expands outward and upward. Begin to circulate power and energy through this coil by drawing in power from your source. Many people think of this power as coming from their higher selves or souls, or from a higher power that might be called the Universal Mind, God, or the All-That-Is. Use as the source of power whatever feels right to you. You might imagine spinning your magnetic coil in whatever direction feels most comfortable.

4. As you think of what you want to magnetize, make your coil whatever size you think it will need to be to draw what you want to you. Does it need to be the size of your whole body, or smaller, or larger? How much power do you need to send through the coil to draw what you want to you? Use your imagination and play with the size, shape, and intensity of the coil until it *feels* just right. As you do this you are beginning to generate a magnetic force field around you, magnetizing what you want to you, much as a magnet draws iron to it.

5. As you draw what you want to you, evaluate where to bring it into your energy. This may be a specific place in

your body. You might imagine a cord going out from your heart, your throat, or your mind, linking with what you want and drawing it to you. You may want to imagine it coming into your hands. Or, it may feel more comfortable to disperse this thing all around you. For instance, a large sum of money may affect many areas of your life; thus when you draw it to you, you might want to imagine it all around you rather than in a specific place.

6. As your coil builds, imagine what events need to occur before you have this thing that you want. There are a certain number of steps you will take and events that will occur to get what you want. You can control the rate at which those events and steps occur, be it one, two, or fifty a day. Begin to work with the time element in manifesting by getting a feeling or picture of how many steps and events are involved. Try speeding up, or slowing down, the rate at which you take these steps and have these events occur, until the rate feels just right. If you are attracting this thing or sum of money too quickly, you will feel a sense of tension or pressure. There is a rate of change that is just right for you.

7. Observe your posture and breathing, and notice that you can increase your feeling of being magnetic by slightly altering each.

8. Continue generating your magnetic coil until you reach a point that feels like a completion of energy. You may feel a "click" or a stop, or the energy may start fading. You may have a feeling of certainty that you will get what you are magnetizing. Stop magnetizing when you feel this certainty. You will notice that the energy builds, crests, and then begins to fall away. Build your magnetic coil and magnetize as long as it feels good. If it becomes a struggle or strain, if it feels like there is a barrier, stop; you have done enough. Discover what is the right amount of energy to put out to draw what you want to you.

9. Now go within and ask your higher self how often to magnetize what you have asked for.

10. Come gently out of this state and stretch your body. Over the next several days notice if you have any insights about this object and how you might get it.

Evaluation:

Keep doing this exercise until you are able to feel, visualize, sense, imagine, or experience the coil and the energy you are sending out. If you are able to feel the energy build and then retreat, or if you are able to feel a click or sense of completion, or have a feeling that the building energy has receded, you have begun the process of drawing in what you want. When you feel comfortable with magnetizing a small object, use this exercise for magnetizing something that is a greater challenge for you. You may notice that every time you magnetize something your coil changes. Sometimes your coil and the amount of energy you circulate through it is small; sometimes you need a larger coil and more energy. Sometimes you will want to magnetize for at least a minute or longer, and sometimes a few seconds will be enough. Remember to hold positive thoughts about what you request and to have a certain detachment about receiving it. Let it be all right if it comes in a different form than what you expect; surrender to having whatever comes as being appropriate for you to have.

EXERCISE:

Magnetizing a Person You Don't Yet Know

You can use this exercise to draw to you a person you don't yet know. This is best done with people such as potential employers, employees, mechanics, and others you will have working relationships with. (This exercise is not designed to magnetize soul-mates or intimate relationships.)

Preparation:

Find a time and place where you can relax and think without interruption for a few minutes. Relax and prepare yourself in the same way as in the *Learning to Relax* exercise on page 14.

Steps:

1. Think about the person you want to magnetize. Think about or list all the qualities this ideal person would have. Don't leave anything out. What attitudes will he or she have? What skills and knowledge? How will you relate? Be as complete and specific as possible.

2. Now create a scene in which you imagine yourself interacting with this person, or imagine the good feelings you will have about this person.

3. Imagine that you have a power source within your heart area that generates energy. Then picture a coil, like a loop, that goes around and around. This coil begins in the area near your heart inside your body and expands outward and upward. Begin to circulate power and energy through this coil by drawing on your power source. Spin your magnetic coil in whatever direction feels most comfortable.

4. As you begin to circulate power and energy through this coil let go of any neediness. You can magnetize out of neediness, but it dilutes your effectiveness Detach and sur-

render to having the best person come. Know that you cannot force anyone to do anything against his or her will, and that you can draw someone to you only if it is for the higher good of both of you.

5. As you energize the coil and send it out from your heart, think about the ideal person you have described. Imagine that you are connecting with him or her telepathically. As you link imagine that you have the ability to communicate with this ideal person's soul. Begin to connect with them, mentally appreciating the person for all the good he or she will bring into your life. Tell this person telepathically how you will bring good into his or her life as well.

6. As you put energy through your coil, make it as large as you think it needs to be, and add love to the energy in the coil. You are sending a welcoming, inviting feeling. The more love you send, the more magnetic you become. Imagine you are looking at the soul of this person, or perhaps just seeing his or her eyes. Feel the magnetism you are generating through linking your heart with his or her heart. Ask that the highest good be created for both of you in your connection.

7. Begin to feel this person coming into your energy field, as if they were coming from a dream and walking into your reality, until you can almost sense them in front of you. Thank the person in advance for assisting you.

8. Observe your posture and breathing, and notice you can increase your feeling of being magnetic by slightly altering each.

9. Keep magnetizing, sending love, and drawing this person to you until you feel a completion or a click. Sometimes you will get an immediate feeling of connection, as if this person is right there. At other times it may feel as if you are reaching out into a void; when this happens, take another look at whom you think you want to connect with. It may mean that your timing is off or you need to think things through more thoroughly. There is usually a fairly strong, recognizable

click when you have made a connection to the person you seek.

10. Now go within and ask your higher self how often to magnetize this person.

11. Come gently out of this state and stretch your body. Over the next several days notice if you have any insights about this person and how you might contact them.

Evaluation:

It may take practice to draw in exactly the right person, as well as a willingness to allow yourself to believe you deserve to be served by others. Keep doing this exercise until you are able to feel, visualize, sense, imagine, or experience the coil and the energy you are sending out. If you are able to feel the energy build and then retreat, or if you are able to feel a sense of completion or a click, you have made contact and begun the process of attracting the person you want.

One woman who used this exercise to magnetize someone to help her with her errands and housework continually attracted people who wanted her to take care of them rather than vice versa. She realized that she believed that she didn't deserve to be served by others. She worked with this belief by affirming that she did deserve to have wonderful help. Soon she attracted a woman who is perfect for the job and is still with her. Remember that the people you draw to you will be your mirrors. If you are always too tired to honor your higher path, you may draw people to you who are too tired to do good work for you. You may notice a pattern in the people you attract. For example, if you often attract mechanics who don't treat you with respect, you may not be treating yourself with respect, and they may only be mirroring your pattern back to you. Change the pattern within yourself and then use this exercise again to draw to you the person you want to connect with.

EXERCISE:
_____

Magnetizing a Number of People

You can use this exercise to magnetize clients for your business, people to interest in a project, or people you can serve or assist in some way.

Preparation:

Find a time and place where you can relax and think without interruption for a few minutes. Relax and prepare yourself in the same way as in the *Learning to Relax* exercise on page 14. As this exercise uses skills and images developed in the *General Magnetizing* and *Magnetizing a Person You Don't Yet Know* exercises, do this exercise only after you have already completed those exercises.

Steps:

1. Think of the people you want to magnetize. Think about or list all the qualities these people will have. What are their interests? How can you serve them? What feelings do you have as you think of them? How will you relate to them? Be as complete and specific as possible.

2. Now create a scene in which you imagine yourself interacting with these people, or in which you live out the good feelings you will have about them.

3. Generate your magnetic coil from your heart. First make it as large as your body, then as large as you feel drawn to make it. Imagine you are sending out a call from your heart to the souls of all those people who may be assisted by your work. Feel yourself drawing them to you. Tell them telepathically how you will make a contribution to their lives with whatever you are offering them. (For instance, if you are selling a product, mentally tell them all the ways that product will assist them in making their lives better.) When you are focused upon serving or assisting people you are very magnetic. Ask

for people who value and honor your work, for it is better to attract one person who honors your work rather than three who do not. Do not focus on what people will give you or what you want from them, for you are not magnetic when you do. Be aware of what you will offer these people that will serve their higher good, and magnetize with this thought in mind.

4. As you begin to circulate power and energy through your coil let go of any neediness. Detach and surrender to having whomever would benefit and is attracted to your work come to you. Know that you cannot force anyone to do anything against his or her will, and that you can only draw people to you when it is for the higher good of all parties concerned.

5. As you energize the coil and send it out from your heart, think about the people you have described. Thank these people in advance for your opportunity to serve them. As you put more energy through your coil or make it larger and larger, imagine it reaching out through your city, state, entire country, or the whole world.

6. Imagine that as people connect with you they are like light bulbs lighting up. See hundreds, then thousands, of lights being turned on all around you. Imagine that lines of light reach back and forth between you and all the people you will reach. How does this feel? Make your vision as real and as inventive as you can. For instance, if you are magnetizing people to reach with your work, imagine what you will feel like when you are reaching ten new people a week. Sense their energy; let it be a part of your reality. How will your life change when you reach this number of people? Now imagine reaching twenty-five new people a week with your work.

7. Continue imagining connecting with more and more people. Imagine fifty, one hundred, or even more new people a week tuning into your work and being helped by it in some way.

8. As you connect with more and more people, feel the changes that this will make in your life. As you imagine more and more people, adjust your mental pictures to comfortably include this number of people. If it doesn't feel comfortable at first, keep imagining this connection in different ways until it does. The more easily you can imagine this the more easily you can make it a reality. Ask for the lifestyle, business structures, and assistance you will need to handle this many people connecting with your work.

9. Observe your posture and breathing, and notice you can increase your feeling of being magnetic by slightly altering each.

10. Stop at whatever level feels most comfortable. Know that at each level you will have the proper setup to make connecting with this number of people acceptable and joyful to you.

11. Now go within and ask your higher self how often to magnetize.

12. Come gently out of this state and stretch your body. Over the next several days notice if you have any insights about these people and how you might connect with them.

Evaluation:

Notice what number of people you reached before you were no longer able to imagine a connection. Visualize connecting with slightly less than that number of people and make the feeling as joyful, light, and easy as possible. When you are ready, move up to a larger number. As you learn to feel comfortable with larger numbers of people, you will be creating the necessary changes in your energy to bring these people into your life.

EXERCISE:

Group Magnetizing

One of the most powerful magnetizing techniques is getting together with others and sending energy to each person to create what he or she is asking for. The energy of a group magnifies many times the ability to create money, objects, events, and forms. A group holding a common thought can make that thought a reality even more powerfully than an individual.

Preparation:

This exercise can be done anywhere, including a public place such as a restaurant. Before starting, pick someone to lead the exercise. The role of this person is to keep the circle moving and to assist people in getting clear about what they are asking for.

Steps:

1. The leader starts by explaining to the group the following procedure: Each person asks for only one thing at a time. The group then magnetizes what that person has requested. This may be followed by a brief comment by anyone who would like to comment, depending on the time available.

2. The leader then asks everyone in the group to get quiet for a moment and decide upon one specific thing to ask for. When the group is ready, the leader picks one person to start.

3. As each person in turn tells the group what they would like the group to assist them in magnetizing, the leader balances between helping the person be as clear as possible about the request and keeping a smooth and flowing pace. The most successful results come from requests for something specific, something that for that person seems possible to have. For instance, a person who asks for money will want to be as

specific as possible, such as stating how much money per month is wanted. If the request is vague, for instance if someone asks for happiness, the leader might ask how they would know if they had happiness. This will help them recognize what they are asking for when it comes. If the request is for something that is hard to visualize, or the person doesn't know clearly what they want, the person making the request may want to think of a symbol that would represent what they have requested, and everyone would focus on that symbol. The leader will assist each person in being brief and focused; if someone talks too long it could dispel the group energy.

4. After someone states a request, everyone closes their eyes and sends this person energy. During this time, the person who is asking for something might want to think of how having this object, sum of money, or whatever will benefit both their and others' higher good. This person will want to think of the essence of their request and feel the higher quality, such as love, peace, aliveness, and joy, that having it will bring as they are sent energy by the group.

5. There are an infinite number of ways to send energy to someone. Use your imagination and do whatever feels good. Be playful and imaginative with your pictures. The first time a group uses this exercise, the leader can explain that it only takes a moment for the energy to be received. The leader monitors the energy as it is being sent. You will probably feel the energy come to a peak, then start falling. This usually happens within 3 to 5 seconds. When the energy starts falling away, the leader calls an end, perhaps by saying "Thank you."

6. People are often so enthusiastic after sending energy to someone that they want to discuss what they saw and the insights they received afterward. If there is time, you may want to have a brief comment period after each person has been sent energy to share insights and experiences. This can also be done once for the entire group after all requests have been magnetized. The leader monitors the time spent on feed-

back to ensure that it is in keeping with a high level of energy and a smoothly flowing pace.

7. When one person's request is complete, the leader asks the next person to state his or her request. You can go around the group and magnetize requests as often as you would like. The leader makes sure that if another cycle is started the energy is still high.

Evaluation:

At the end of a group manifesting session you will have generated a lot of energy. You might want to offer that energy to mankind; the animal, plant, and mineral kingdoms; or the universe. Simply sit together quietly and imagine you are dispersing the extra energy you have generated to all the kingdoms to be used for their good. The more energy you send out, the more energy will come back to you.

Developing Mastery

Following Your Inner Guidance

Allowing Success

Transforming Your Beliefs

Letting Money Flow

Coming Out of Survival

Trusting

Miracles

CHAPTER 5

Following
Your Inner Guidance

Learn to listen to your inner guidance. After you have worked with energy and magnetized what you want, your inner guidance will lead you to it in the quickest, simplest way. When you listen to and act upon your guidance, you follow your natural flow of energy. It is that effortless, easy flow that leads you to all the things you have been asking for. Inner guidance comes from your higher self and speaks to you in the form of feelings, insights, and inner knowing. Inner guidance brings you information from sources other than those that can be detected by your physical senses. By getting quiet and listening to your thoughts and feelings, you can tap into a much larger spectrum of information than is ordinarily thought to be available.

As your thoughts about what you want go out into the universe, your higher self looks over past, present, and future events; it views the connections and the situations that will need to be created for you to have what you ask for. It then finds the best way to bring them to you. It begins drawing to you certain people, opportunities, and events. It creates opportunities for you to meet people who might assist you and will also benefit from knowing you, for the universe works for the greater good of all. Your feelings signal what actions to take. Your willingness to be spontaneous, follow inner urges and hunches, and listen to strong feelings and act upon them will lead you to your goals.

I *trust and follow my inner guidance.*

Inner guidance directs you to your higher good. Learning to distinguish inner guidance from wishful or fearful thinking is one of your challenges. If an urge feels joyful or delightful to follow, it probably comes from your inner guidance. If the results you are hoping for seem to be too good to be true or if you suspect yourself of wishful thinking, it is probably not inner guidance. Honor your inner sense and spend time checking out the details. Ask, "Is this my true inner guidance? Does it feel right and good; or am I just hoping?"

Since your soul speaks to you through your feelings and thoughts, the more you are aware of them the easier it will be to hear and develop your inner guidance. If your thoughts or feelings are unusual for the circumstance, pay attention to them. You develop your inner guidance when you act upon your inner messages and get feedback.

For instance, as you are getting ready to go to a store you might have the thought or feeling you ought to call first to see if it is open. You don't usually have this feeling or thought; you simply go. In this case, you call and check, only to find the store is closed for remodeling. As you get in the habit of paying attention to and acting on your feelings and thoughts, it will get easier to distinguish between what is inner guidance and what is not.

To manifest things easily, even before you know you need them, follow your feelings and inner messages. Start in small ways by saying "no" when you mean "no," and "yes" when you mean "yes." Ask yourself throughout the day, "Is this what I feel like doing? Is this the lightest and most joyful activity for me, or am I making myself do it because I think I have to?" Trust that your feelings of joy, delight, and self-love are always leading you toward your higher good.

There are several kinds of inner guidance. One kind is a negative sense or even a warning about an action you are thinking of taking. Another kind gives you insights about future paths or directions you might choose. Another helps you be in the right place at the right time, creating through coincidences and synchronicity the events you need to get you where you are going as easily as possible.

The kind of inner guidance that gives you warning signals usually comes through your emotions and is often experienced as a feeling of anxiety or an uncomfortable feeling in the "pit" of your stomach. One man who was a stock market investor said he knew when he had made a bad investment because he felt more tense and anxious than usual after making a buy. You can develop your awareness of this kind of guidance by knowing how you normally feel, and paying attention to unusual anxiety or nervousness. This man knew what his normal level of tension was after making an investment, so he was aware when he was unusually tense. Your challenge will be to learn the difference between your normal fears and those inner emotional messages that are your higher guidance.

I *spend quiet reflective time;*
I hear my inner guidance.

Inner guidance about your future path and directions often comes to you when you are in a quiet, reflective state, performing activities that take you out of your normal awareness. This kind of guidance can be a thought, feeling, picture, or daydream of what you would like to be doing. It may grow and build on itself each time you get quiet. You can develop this kind of guidance by giving yourself more time to sit quietly, relaxing your body, and reflecting on your life. Performing creative or athletic activities can also trigger this kind of intuition. You may get sudden and unexpected insights into your life while you are painting, drawing, playing or creating music, running, or swimming. Take action on this guidance; if you constantly avoid acting on the guidance you get, it will become harder and harder to hear or recognize future guidance.

When you get an idea, don't over-analyze it, asking "Is this idea going to create my new path, be profitable, or support me for the rest of my life?" Ideas are like seeds; when they first come up you often don't know what they're going to grow into. Just keep following your joyful impulses, and your ideas will unfold into the forms that best serve you.

I am always in the right place at the right time.

The kind of inner guidance that leads you to being in the right place at the right time comes from knowing your normal thoughts and paying attention to those that are different. For instance, you usually drive a certain route to work, but one day you have a thought to drive a different way. You may have had the same thought before, but this day you recognize that there is a sense of urgency about it. You go the new way, and as you drive you hear on the radio about a traffic jam along the route you normally take. There will be a subtly different quality or feeling to those thoughts that are coming from your higher guidance. You can learn to recognize what is inner guidance and what isn't by taking action on those subtle feelings and thoughts and by observing the results.

As another example, you have been wanting to buy a certain item but have been unable to find it. You might have spent several days calling all around or shopping at many stores, to no avail. One day you get a picture in your mind of a certain store and a feeling to go there, even though it isn't a store you normally shop at. You pay attention to this unusual urge and go to the store. The item you have been looking for has just arrived and you are able to purchase it. In looking back, you realize that you did not have a real urge or picture to go to all the other stores you checked out. You might have gone shopping because you hoped what you wanted would be there, ignoring the fact that your feelings and pictures were not guiding you to those stores.

Sometimes it is better to wait and take no action until you have a feeling, thought, or picture about what action to take. Waiting for guidance on what action to take eliminates unnecessary work and helps you be in the right place at the right time, creating things you want easily and effortlessly.

Think of something you want. Are there any actions that come to mind that you could take to get what you want? It may be something very simple, such as making a phone call or going to a store that comes to mind if you want to buy something. Are you willing to take that action? Decide when you will do it. If you receive no guidance at this time be willing not to take any action, but follow your joy from moment to moment. Pay more attention than usual to your thoughts about this item, so that when a picture of what action to take comes, you will be aware of it. Take the time, every time you think of what you want, to get quiet and notice what pictures come to mind of action you could take.

Your soul's urges, true inner guidance hunches, are concerned with something you are already familiar with directly or indirectly. These urges give you both the ideas and the momentum to carry them out. If you have a sudden urge to do something that you know nothing about, that would take months to do properly, and you don't have the time, it is probably a passing fancy, not inner guidance. The actions your inner guidance urges you to take are the logical next steps for you, or are steps you can carry out with the knowledge you now have. Sometimes you will have an urge to acquire new information, and later the guidance to take action based on that information will come. There is seldom urgency connected with such directives; you are given plenty of time to carry them out at a pace that is comfortable for you.

One way to develop and hear your inner guidance is to look back at past successes and ask, "What feelings and thoughts did I have at the time I made that decision to take action?" Think of something you bought that you feel was an excellent purchase. Can you remember how you felt about buying it? Even though you may have had moments of indecision, there may have been an inner "knowing" that guided you. If you go back and view your decisions to spend money on something that did not work out well, you will probably be able to remember that your "inner sense" was different from when you were pleased with what you bought.

If a situation occurs that you don't like, you can look back and examine what feelings or thoughts you may have had that were trying to lead you in another direction. You are constantly receiving guidance from your higher self about how to achieve results in the simplest, most joyful way possible. Be very alert to hear this guidance. Develop the habit of paying close attention to your thoughts and feelings before you act. Get to know how you normally think and feel so you can recognize subtle changes. As you do you will become more alert and aware of the guidance you are constantly receiving.

I *follow my highest joy.*

Whenever you feel a heaviness, a resistance, or a reluctance to continue, it is a sign that you are not following your highest path. Your higher self speaks to you by making you feel joyful when you follow your higher path, and resistant and heavy when you don't. If you are forcing yourself to do things according to a list of "shoulds," you are not listening to the deeper part of your being. Your soul rarely says, "You must do this; you should do that." Your soul says, "Isn't this delightful? Doesn't this bring you great joy? Wouldn't you love to do more of it?"

You have all experienced times when you resisted taking an action but didn't know why, and later found out that the act was unnecessary or inappropriate. You may have had a project to do and resisted working on it. Following your inner guidance and feelings of joy, you put it aside and worked on something else. Later that day or that week you might have received a call and found out that the situation had changed; the project was no longer necessary or a different action was required. If you had "forced" yourself to work on the project you would have had to do it all over again.

It is good to temporarily set aside all the activities you have been telling yourself you *should* do and ask yourself what you would *like* to do. By following your inner guidance and joyful feelings, you save yourself unnecessary work.

I *honor myself in everything I do.*

Some resistance can be self-sabotage. It comes from feeling that you aren't worthy of having more than you have. If you know deep inside that a healthy diet, exercise, handling an issue, or some other course of action would truly benefit you, but you resist, you may need to learn to honor yourself more. Rather than confronting the bigger issues immediately, first take small actions that honor you. Think of something really nurturing and luxurious you would like to do for yourself. Perhaps you would like to soak in a warm bath, buy flowers for your house, or take a half hour for yourself every day.

Taking the time to do nurturing activities gives your

subconscious a message that you are a worthy person who deserves to have your goals met. It will be easier to do some of the larger steps that honor you if you build up to them by doing smaller steps. And it will be easier to follow the inner directions that emerge once you build a habit of honoring your deeper needs and feelings.

There will be times when your inner guidance will say, "I want to work all day. It feels so good to accomplish all that I am accomplishing." Your inner guidance will not always lead you to instant gratification; it often pursues a longer-range sense of inner accomplishment and satisfaction. Inner guidance speaks in many different ways, but always through a sense of self-love and feeling good about what you are doing.

If you are forcing yourself to do something, working at a job out of obligation or spending money because you feel you have to, you are not listening to your inner guidance. If you are in a job where you must force yourself to do many tasks you don't want to do, look at the larger picture. Why are you in a job that doesn't allow you to do what you enjoy doing? If you love your job and most of what you are doing, but dislike several tasks, look again at those areas. There may be a better way to do them, perhaps a better procedure, a different job division between you and a co-worker, or ways your family, children, or friends could help. Pay attention to your negative feelings—they have messages for you about how your situation could be better.

You do not honor yourself by working for hours at activities that are not joyful. If you do what is joyful, you may find that all the jobs you are forcing yourself to do to make money are no longer necessary. You will also discover that you make more money in the long run by doing what you love than by doing things you don't love.

The more you feel joyful when you do things and follow your urges, hunches, and higher vision, the more quickly and easily you will get what you ask for. As you follow your higher path, the more you will find everything working in miraculous and easy ways. This is not to say that you won't be challenged, for challenges help you to gain strength and confidence. Your dreams will come true as you follow your feelings of joy, delight, and self-love.

EXERCISE:

Linking Up with the Higher Forces

You do not need to do this exercise frequently. Do it whenever you want to feel more connected to your inner guidance from your higher self or soul, or to the current of mankind's evolution, or to strengthen your link to the higher forces of the universe. Some people view these higher forces as God, the All-That-Is, Buddha, Christ, the Universal Mind, or the Higher Will. Every time you do this exercise you are building a bridge of light upward. Doing this exercise before you magnetize something that is big or represents a quantum leap for you will add to your power to attract it.

Preparation:

Find a quiet time alone. This exercise need only take a few minutes, and can be repeated whenever you want.

Steps:

1. Close your eyes and envision yourself building a bridge of light upward to the higher planes of reality. You might picture a beam of light coming out of the top of your head and going straight up as high as you can imagine.

2. Imagine that you are connecting with the source of all life, drinking in energy and light until every cell in your body is aglow with light and energy.

3. Picture your mind as a clear mountain lake, with every cell clearly reflecting the higher planes of reality. Imagine that every thought and every cell in your mind is now linked to the higher mind, the universal mind, the All-That-Is. As you keep imagining this link, you are creating it as real.

4. Imagine that you are aligning your will with the Higher Will. You might envision a cord of light coming out of your solar plexus, the area above your navel, and linking with the source of all life you connected with in Step 2.

5. Picture this source energy as a golden globe of energy and light, six inches above your head. Slowly bring this globe down through your body, letting it align all the energy in your body with its higher light. Keep moving it through your body until you are standing on it. Envision it beaming light and energy from below your feet back up through you. Then bring it back up through your body and let it sit about six inches above your head.

6. Visualize your soul as a cool blue flame, either within or outside of you. Let that flame grow steadily and brightly, growing larger and larger as you are filled with the energy of your soul. In your mind's eye, approach this cool blue flame of your soul and ask for a deeper, more conscious connection to it. Your soul always hears your sincere requests and will immediately begin helping you have a stronger connection to its guidance and direction.

7. Now bring your awareness and attention to the top of your head, and imagine that you have an antenna. This energy center is where telepathic communication from the higher dimensions occurs. You can receive any broadcast you wish by intending to do so and using your imagination to establish the link. There is a telepathic broadcast of mankind's path of highest evolution. Mentally adjust your imaginary antenna to pick up this broadcast. As you do, you will be aligning your actions with the current of mankind's evolution. All that you manifest will be more in alignment with your and others' higher purpose.

8. When you are ready, open your eyes and enjoy the feeling of connection to the higher realms.

Evaluation:

Be imaginative with this exercise and create new pictures and images to strengthen your connection to the higher realms. As you imagine this connection, you are creating it as your reality. We have used many images; remember that they are designed to give you an experience of the higher energies and your soul. What is most important is your experience of the connection and not the images we have used. After you have felt this connection, you can recreate it any way you want using whatever images, thoughts, or pictures help you achieve it.

CHAPTER 6

*A*llowing *S*uccess

As you magnetize what you want and follow your inner guidance, you will want to allow success into your life so you can receive what you have asked for. Mastering manifesting involves learning to make those choices and decisions that hold the most light for you and put you onto your higher path. As you choose the path of most light, you are also choosing success at its highest levels. You create the reality you experience by the choices and decisions you make.

What you have and where you are today are the results of all the choices and decisions you have made. Many of your choices have been passive, made without conscious examination. Many have been based on your past programming rather than on your new unlimited thinking. You can begin now to make more conscious, aware choices. Acknowledge that where you are today is a result of your past choices, and realize that at every moment you are truly creating your reality. If you are not happy with what you have created so far, you can learn to make different choices and change your life into one that brings you joy, aliveness, or whatever else you want.

I always choose the path of most light.

Some choices are subtle, but there is usually one alternative that carries more light, that will put you on a slightly higher path and help you express your essence more clearly than the others. By choosing your higher path you will accelerate your growth, aliveness, and abundance. It is important to develop your ability to discriminate and choose the path of most light to create abundance in your life.

One woman who had been making jewelry for a long time decided that she wanted to distribute her jewelry to a larger market by putting it in stores across the country. Her jewelry contained many esoteric symbols, and she wanted it to be widely available to people who would be assisted by wearing the healing symbols. She thought of getting friends to help her distribute the jewelry, but every time she started in that direction it seemed difficult and her heart wasn't in it. It would require financial resources and skills she didn't have, and would leave her no time to make new jewelry. Because that path didn't seem joyful, she rejected it and asked for inner guidance about a better way. She got the idea to ask stores how they bought other people's jewelry. She discovered that an entire distribution system already existed, complete with sales representatives who were happy to handle her jewelry. She found the highest path by making choices and decisions that supported doing what she loved.

When you have a choice to make and the highest option is not immediately obvious, ask yourself a series of questions. If all choices look equally good, ask, "Which decision holds the most joy for me? Which seems to call to my heart as something I would love to do?" Then pick the option that brings you the most joy. Even if the joyful path does not appear to promise you as much money, in the long run it will be far more profitable than the choice that isn't as joyful. Don't make your choice based on how much money it appears you will make; following the path of your heart will always bring you more abundance.

If all choices seem equally joyful, ask, "Which choice makes the most sense to follow and is the most practical for me right now?" Your highest path will always make practical sense. If the choices are still equal, ask "Which choice makes the greatest contribution to mankind or allows me the greatest opportunity to serve others?" If both choices still look equal, think of the higher qualities you want to create in your life, such as well-being, love, and aliveness. Which choice allows you to express these qualities more fully?

It is wiser not to put yourself in a position where you have to make immediate decisions without time to thoroughly think things out. If you do find yourself in a situation where you need to make a decision quickly, imagine that you are holding one choice in your right hand and one in your left hand. Ask the hand that holds the higher choice to raise itself.

I *honor my integrity in all that I do.*

The purity and integrity of your energy is very important, for your integrity guides you to create those things that are in harmony with the deepest part of your being. Your integrity leads you to those choices and situations that are prosperous for you. You know when you are maintaining your integrity and when you are not. If you feel that you are com promising your ideals, doing something for money that does not feel comfortable to you, you are not operating within your integrity. Honor your integrity and you will be repaid many times over with increased prosperity.

It is important to feel good about everything you do, to act upon your values, to be honest with the people you deal with, and to come from your truth. Your integrity challenges you to look at what is real and important to you, and to choose that over illusions, promises, and glamour. Come from your highest ideals, follow your own wisdom over another person's, and do things in ways that honor you and feel right to you. Honor everyone you deal with and hold everything you do up to the light of your soul. Your energy and being are your gifts to the world. The more your energy is clear and flowing, the more you have to give others. Money that you create from your integrity is money of light that will bring good to you and others.

I *am a success.*
I allow myself to feel successful.

To develop your mastery of abundance more quickly, start by recognizing how successful you already are at creating what you want, at honoring your integrity, and at making good choices. Build on what you know you can do. Thank and love yourself for the strength and vision you have right now. Take a moment to tell yourself you are already a success. You can feel successful right now, without depending on meeting certain goals to give that feeling to you. You can recognize all the wonderful things you are already doing in your life.

Success comes from feeling successful in the present moment; it is not something you may feel some day when you have reached a goal or have something you want. Don't think that large sums of money will create that feeling for you; people with a lot of money rarely feel successful unless they have learned how to appreciate themselves and feel successful from within.

Rather than define success in terms of the concrete things it might represent to you such as how much money you would have in the bank, what type of house you would live in, or what type of car you would drive, be willing to expand your definition of success to include the goals of your higher self. True success is having the right amount of money, transforming an old habit or negative belief, releasing a fear, doing things you love, and developing and recognizing your special talents. From a higher point of view, success is creating something when you need it, making a contribution to others, and loving and respecting yourself and others. It is growing and learning from all your experiences. Look at others as successful not by how rich they are, but by the quality and happiness of their lives. As you focus on these higher qualities of success, you will realize that in terms of your higher self you have already achieved many successes, even if you haven't yet met the specific financial goals set by your personality.

I *congratulate myself often.*

The essence of success for most people is a feeling of self-love, self-esteem, or self-worth. See if you can capture that feeling for a moment. Say to yourself, "I am a success." How does it feel? Can you capture that feeling for several moments and let it radiate throughout your body? Acknowledge all the successful things you are doing right now. As you acknowledge your success in other areas, it becomes easier to view yourself as successful with money. Your body is your vehicle for manifestation, for it creates the actions that bring your thoughts and emotions into form. As you bring the feeling of success into your body more frequently, this feeling will draw further success to you in every area of your life.

Appreciate where you are now. Rather than focusing on how far you have to go, appreciate how far you have come. As you look at the long-term goals you want to create it is good to define small, discernible steps along the way. Then, as you reach each step, you can tell the little child inside you, "Congratulations. Job well done! I have come a long way toward my goal." When you reach a goal you have been striving for, give yourself a reward before you look to the next goal. Some people look ahead to the next mountain without taking time to appreciate the one they have just climbed. They never have the satisfied feeling they are looking for. Acknowledge your successes, for as you do you will build upon them.

View yourself as successful in the past as well as the present and future. Think of a time in the past when you felt like a success. Remember those circumstances and feelings. The more you remember past successes, the more you will create success in the future. Look back at how you have handled yourself in the past, and see that there was higher wisdom in all of your choices. Some choices led you to grow, some led you to change your life, and all were the best you knew how to make at the time. Even though you may not have understood why you made certain choices, those choices still assisted you.

As you look back from the perspective of your now-wiser self, you can see that even choices you thought were bad taught you much and made you the person you are today. If you are not happy with your circumstances right now, realize that you can make new choices from now on and begin to change your circumstances for the better.

I *forgive myself, knowing that I did the best I knew how at the time.*

Forgive yourself when you look back into the past and think of things like, "I didn't spend my money wisely. I should have bought that property and now I'd have lots of money. I shouldn't have made that investment that didn't turn out well. I shouldn't have lent that money to a friend; I knew I'd never get it back." Those kinds of thoughts can hold you back from greater abundance. Drop your pictures of times in the past when situations didn't work out as well as you wanted. If those thoughts arise, do not pay attention to them, but think instead of when you did spend your money wisely, were happy with what you got, made a good return on your money, or were paid back in full by a friend. As you forgive and love your past self, focusing on all the times you have succeeded, you change the course of your future.

Take a moment and look at your childhood messages. How did your parents spend money? Did they buy things for themselves? Did they enjoy their money, or did they struggle to have enough? Did they talk freely with you about how much they earned, or was money a forbidden topic? How did they spend on you? Did you feel that your wishes counted? Can you see a connection between the way you relate to money now and the relationship your parents had to money? Did your parents allow themselves to spend and earn money in ways that brought them aliveness, happiness, well-being, and self-love?

I *give myself permission
to have what I want.*

Children are accustomed to receiving things from their parents, and many people expect to receive from the universe in the way they received from their parents. If your parents were generous and giving, you may believe in a generous and giving universe. If your parents denied you many of the things you wanted, you may still be denying yourself the things you want. You may be acting as if you are waiting for some invisible "parent" or outside authority to decide whether or not you can have what you want. Are you acting as if the universe is your parent? Be the parent that would now be appropriate for you to have, give yourself permission to have whatever you want.

You can create a new personal history for yourself, focusing on all the times you were successful and did have a measure of abundance. Let go of stories of your past that do not support the new picture of success and abundance you are creating. The images you hold of the past often put limits on the future you can imagine for yourself, and thus keep you from manifesting your greater potential.

To release the past, look at the stories you have been telling yourself and others about your childhood and money. Do you tell people that you had abundance or scarcity? Perhaps you tell about the times when there wasn't enough food. Or perhaps you tell tales about how your parents spent money, but didn't buy things for you. Start by looking at the aspects of your personal history you emphasize with others. For every experience you had, you also had an experience that was nearly its opposite. There were times you had wonderful meals and times you got things you really wanted that had value to you.

What financial history would you like to have? Begin to make a new history for yourself. Reconstruct your childhood with memories of prosperity and getting what you wanted. What would you like to tell people your childhood was like? For instance, you might want to tell people, "My parents spent money very wisely. Money was not an issue in our family; we always had enough." As you say this you will probably remember times when money really wasn't an issue and you really did have enough.

You have had the elements of every experience with money. You have had the experience of feeling abundant, even if just for a moment. Perhaps you got a beautiful toy that you wanted. Perhaps somebody gave you an unexpected gift of money, or you received more than you asked for. The more you capture that sense of joy, enthusiasm, and appreciation, the more good things you will attract in your future.

L*ove getting there*
as much as being there.

ALLOWING SUCCESS
PLAYSHEET

1 | Picture something you want that you don't yet have.

2 | Think of all the reasons why you are now closer to getting what you want than you have ever been.

3 | Take a moment and experience what success feels like to you. You might recall a past or present success or imagine what a future success will feel like. Let it become as physical and as emotional an experience as you can. Find the posture and breathing that success brings for you. Breathe in that success for a few moments. Congratulate yourself on all the things you can think of that you are doing well right now.

4 | One way you can allow success is by telling your personal history in a way that emphasizes all the good experiences you have had. You can play the following game alone or with friends. Come up with answers in three minutes or less. As you describe your past in a new way, that becomes your new reality.

a. Tell your personal history as if you grew up with great abundance. Pick actual incidents, focusing only on times when you felt abundant, got what you wanted, or experienced your parents as abundant. You will be amazed at how many times you can remember when you did feel abundant.

b. Tell your personal history from the perspective of how you know you have always been divinely guided, as if you had a guardian angel. Think of two or three incidents to demonstrate this.

c. Tell your personal history from the perspective of how easily you have created things you wanted, perhaps remembering a time when you wanted something and it appeared quickly, without any effort on your part.

See how good it feels to focus on the areas of your past that worked for you. The more you focus on the abundance you had in the past, the more prosperity you will create in the future. Energy follows thought. Whatever you pay attention to grows and increases. If you pay attention to your past successes, you will create a successful, positive future for yourself.

CHAPTER 7

Transforming Your Beliefs

Your beliefs create your reality. Beliefs are assumptions about the nature of reality, and because you create what you believe in, you will have many "proofs" that reality operates the way you think it does. For instance, a person who believes that the universe is abundant will act in such a way that he or she experiences abundance, and a person who believes that money comes only from working hard will receive money only from hard work. Each will have many experiences to prove that their "belief" about reality is really a "fact" about reality. You can change what you believe and thus change what you experience.

After you have magnetized and worked with energy to get what you want, your beliefs will affect how easily and quickly things come to you. To discover a belief, look at a past or present situation in your life. This may be a problem or challenge you are dealing with, or something wonderful you have created. Ask yourself, what would a person who created this have to believe in order to be in this situation? If a person were unable to pay his bills, constantly getting reminders from loan companies and avoiding phone calls because of them, what would he believe about reality to create this circumstance? He might believe that he didn't deserve to have money, that paying bills was a real struggle, or that life was hard.

One common belief is that people won't love you as much if you have money, that they will love you for your money and not for yourself. You may worry that having money will somehow separate you from your friends. Yet, you are rarely deceived into thinking someone loves you unless you want to be deceived. Your worry that you will not be loved if you have money can be healed by feeling from moment to moment the love you have for others. When you give love to others, you will receive love in return. People love you right now, and you have a certain amount of money. Is there a particular sum of money you could have that will make people suddenly stop loving you?

M*y beliefs create my reality.*
I believe in my unlimited prosperity.

Some of you believe that having a large sum of money will become a burdensome responsibility and tie you down. Not being able to pay your bills and worrying about money are also burdens, and can tie you down. You will not be tied down by money unless you believe you will be and set it up so that you are. What you believe is what you create. If you believe that a large sum of money is a burden, it would be good to change that belief before you make a lot of money, or you will experience the money as a burden and a responsibility. If you have asked for a lot of money and don't yet have it, your higher self may be helping you change some of your negative beliefs about having money before it brings you what you have asked for.

Your beliefs about money determine how you attract it, spend it, and relate to it. Do you believe it is possible to make money doing what you love to do? Or do you believe that making money requires hard work and struggle? If there is something you want and you do not yet have it, you may have a belief that is keeping you from having it. Within every belief you are living out there is the seed of the opposite belief that you haven't yet manifested. Within the belief that you don't deserve money lies its opposite—the belief that you DO deserve money. As you take your attention away from the negative belief and begin activating the positive one, you change what you experience.

You may find that some of your limited thinking comes from your parental programming or beliefs. Most of your thoughts, pictures, and concepts were planted at a very early age by the words, beliefs, and unspoken messages of your parents and others you were around. Recognize the beliefs you acquired from your parents, and consciously decide if you want to keep them. Forgive your parents for any beliefs they may have taught you that you no longer want. Realize that they did the best they knew how. In some way those beliefs were perfect for you to have earlier in your life, leading you to the appropriate lessons and growth you needed to achieve more of your potential. You can release any of those old programs and beliefs that no longer serve you, choosing your own operating principles. You can choose what beliefs, thoughts, concepts, and images you want.

I *choose beliefs that bring me aliveness and growth.*

After you discover a belief that is holding you back, let go of it and create a new belief. One way you can do this is to get quiet, close your eyes, imagine light all around you, and in some symbolic way remove the old belief. You may see written out in front of you, "I don't deserve to have money."

Now erase the letters one by one. Picture the new belief in its place, perhaps in big letters: "I deserve money." To further implement a new belief, write it down, say it to yourself when you think of it, and put it where you will see it frequently in your house or at work.

Your emotions and the way you use your imagination either strengthen or weaken the beliefs you have. Do not ignore or deny old beliefs. Accept the old beliefs you discover as your thoughts about the nature of reality, not facts about reality itself. Then imagine yourself having the opposite belief. If you believe that it is hard to make money, imagine that it is easy. Make the picture as real as possible, using your ability to visualize. As you visualize, experience the positive feelings you will have as you live out this new belief. Take one small action each day to remind yourself of your new belief. If you think you don't deserve nice things, buy one really nice thing for yourself. As you take such actions, you may discover new feelings and beliefs coming up for you to see and work with.

M*y beliefs create good things for me.*

You can cultivate new beliefs that will help you accumulate money. For instance, the belief that you can make a living doing what you love might motivate you to be more creative. You might want to believe that money is something to be enjoyed, something that will contribute to your higher purpose and help you make a contribution to mankind. If you believe you are poor, your subconscious will create events that keep you feeling poor. If you believe that wealth is bad, you will keep yourself from using any of the skills and abilities that might bring you money. If you believe that it is better not to have money, you may end up suppressing your talents and skills because expressing them might bring you financial success.

Before you can attract something new, you may need to shift your perception of yourself and your beliefs about deserving to have it. For instance, one woman wanted a new apartment to live in that would be much nicer than her old one. After a year of saving she and her husband were able to afford a much nicer place, and they moved. Because her new home looked more beautiful to her, she began to invite more friends over, dress better, and have better feelings about herself. She thought that the new apartment increased her feelings of self-worth, but she had shifted her perception of herself before she got it. The new place came only after she had made a change in her belief about what she deserved. If she would have seen that what she really wanted was to change her self-image, she would have begun immediately to do those things that brought her the quality of self-worth. The money for the new apartment would have come more rapidly. She had to wait a year because it took her that long to grow into the belief that she was worthy of a better home and deserved to have it.

I *deserve abundance.*

Ask yourself right now, "Is there any reason why I cannot have abundance in my life? Do I deserve it? Do I think that people who have money are in some way more deserving than I am?" Think of all the reasons why it is all right for you to have money.

Think of something you recently received or created that was a reach for you to have. You got this object hoping that it would give you growth and aliveness and a new picture of yourself. What new picture of yourself did this object give you? Before you created this item, you had to change some of your beliefs about who you are and what it is possible for you to have. As you bought or took possession of this item, what new self-image emerged? For example, one man bought a good quality sleeping bag and tent he had been wanting. The new self-image that emerged was of himself as an outdoorsman, as prosperous, and as deserving good equipment. Now, think of something you want that you don't yet have. What new picture of yourself will allow you to have this thing? What new belief about yourself will you need to have to create it? As you create these new beliefs and feelings about yourself, the results of your magnetism will increase dramatically.

TRANSFORMING YOUR BELIEFS
PLAYSHEET

1 | Look at a current situation in your life involving money and ask, "What beliefs would someone have had to create this situation?" List several possibilities. When you have discovered the right one you will know by how you feel inside.

2 | Write below a new belief about money that you would like to have.

3 | Think of something you want. What new belief about yourself might you need to have it?

Note: It often helps to write your new belief on a piece of paper and put it where you will see it frequently. Every time you see this new belief you will be sending energy to it, helping make it a reality.

CHAPTER 8

Letting M oney F low

As you grow and become sensitive to more and more aspects of creating abundance, you will recognize that money flows in and out, like the ocean waves. You will experience times when the tide is in and times when the tide is out. Your universe is made of energy, and energy moves in waves and cycles. There will be times when your magnetism has a larger result and times when it has a smaller result. Some months you will receive more money than usual, and some months you will have more bills than normal. Some weeks your business may be booming, and other weeks you may have very few customers.

There is a natural rhythm to money, just as there is a natural cycle to everything in your life. Every business has an ebb and flow. Every person has cycles in life, times when money is coming in more than it is going out and times when it is going out more than it is coming in. Your challenge is to not go up and down emotionally with the natural ebb and flow of money in your life; use these natural cycles in a way that further builds your prosperity.

M oney flows in my life.
I am prosperous.

There are four basic states of flow you might experience: calm, when money is coming in and going out in equal amounts; flow, when much more money is coming in than going out; ebb, when much more money is going out than coming in; and flat, when no money is flowing in or out. Money represents an exchange of energy between you and the outside world. It represents the energy going out from you and the energy coming back in.

If you are in a calm or flat state, where money is coming in and going out in equal amounts or there isn't any movement, look at where your own energy might not be moving. You want both money and your personal energy to flow. By unblocking your energy, you can create more money in your life. Blocks in money can be caused by places where your energy isn't flowing, such as in your physical body, your emotions, or your relationships with other people. If you are in a calm or flat state with money and you want the energy to begin moving, observe your life for a while and ask your higher self to show you where your energy needs to flow more.

M_y *encrgy is open and flowing in every area of my life.*

Sometimes the lack of flow may be in your body. If your body is not as healthy or as energetic as you would like, you can start having more energy by getting in touch with your inner urgings. Your body is always trying to communicate with you about its needs. What whispers have you been receiving from your body? Perhaps it wants you to get more rest, be out in nature more, get more exercise, or change your diet. Follow your inner urgings and you will gain more physical energy and health. As you gain more flow in this area it will help money to flow in your life. Take a moment to reflect on your body. Is there anywhere you feel physically blocked? Do you have any inner urges that you are not following, such as changing your diet, getting more exercise, getting a massage, or walking outdoors? What simple step could you take today or tomorrow to help open up that area?

Sometimes you may feel emotionally blocked. You may be angry at someone, or suppressing feelings that need to be expressed. You can free emotional blocks by having the intent to go higher and by speaking the truth with compassion. Again, follow your inner urgings; listen to your feelings, honor them, and act upon them. Reflect on your personal relationships. Is there any place where the giving and receiving is not equal, or where you are putting a lot of energy out and getting very little back? Or, are you expecting people to give to you without giving back to them? Do you send out love to other people? Do you feel loved? Is your heart open?

When you observe an area that feels blocked, you can ask, "What specific action can I take to create more flow in this area?" It need not be a major act; it can be simple, such as telling a friend something that needs to be said. What small step could you take in the next week or so to open up the energy between you and someone else? It may be as simple as a phone call, a change in your attitude toward someone, or telling someone telepathically that you accept him or her just as he or she is.

One area in which you are not happy may affect every other area of your life. The more conscious you become of your energy, the less possible it becomes to sweep under the carpet those areas of your life that are not working. To experience the abundance, aliveness, and growth you seek, it is necessary to do what you can to make every area of your life work. When money is not flowing it may be time to start new activities that you have been wanting to do. Look for things you can do that will bring you joy, aliveness, and energy, and start doing them. As you do, you will start your energy moving and create a flow of money.

I *always have more money coming in than going out.*

Everyone looks forward to the flow, when more money is coming in than going out. You experience this many times during each month. When you receive your paycheck or any sum of money, before you spend it, you have created a flow. Start by acknowledging that you already have a flow in your life, and that what you want is even more days when more money is coming in than going out. If you acknowledged yourself every time you had even one day of more money coming in than going out, you would find the flow increasing in your life. If you have reached a level where you consistently have an excess of money coming in, congratulate yourself! You have reached a level of mastery of abundance. Take a moment to appreciate and acknowledge your accomplishment.

There are some challenges at this level. One of the challenges when more money is coming in than going out is to keep your expenses far enough below your increased wealth that when the natural ebb comes you will still be able to pay your bills. Until you completely master the process of manifesting and can create whatever you want at the moment you want it, you may want to save some of your excess money. It is easy at any level of wealth to spend more than you have and keep yourself feeling broke. Some people do not experience abundance because they spend all the money they make or more, or increase their monthly expenses so much when their income goes up that they don't have enough money to meet their bills when the tide goes out. Those who feel wealthy are usually spending less than they make.

One man who was making $15,000 a year began to visualize his monetary success. Within three years he drew in and acted upon enough new business ideas to make in excess of $150,000 a year, working only three days a week. However, in his excitement over having money, he bought a huge new house, a large car, and other expensive items. He quickly increased his monthly expenses to the point where he needed to earn $150,000 just to meet his payments. Even with his increased income, he still felt poor and pressed for money. When business dropped off the next year, he had financial trouble even though he earned $130,000.

I *allow myself to have more than I ever dreamed possible.*

When more money is coming in than going out, when you are getting more business or money than you expected, it is a challenge to continue to ask for more. If you say, "This is too much; if it continues I won't be able to handle all the business, responsibility, or work," you may put the brakes on more tightly than you expect. Then, when the natural ebb comes, you might find the money or business less than you want. When you feel you are being inundated by business, work, opportunities, or money, don't put on the brakes. Challenge yourself to ask for more. Indulge in unlimited thinking and expand your imagination of what it is possible for you to have.

When you are in an upward cycle, keep opening to even more. Realize that as more comes in you will develop new processes, forms, and structures in your life to handle it. You may end up hiring help, changing what you do, and being able to reach more people. As you become more abundant, one of your challenges will be to handle all the choices, opportunities, and abundance that comes to you. You will be challenged to grow, reach more people, get your work out in a larger way, and accept more responsibility, power, and abundance.

LETTING MONEY FLOW
PLAYSHEET

1 | Is there any area in your life that is not working as well as you would like it to work? Take a moment to picture how you would like this area of your life to look. Get quiet and listen to your inner guidance about what you might do to experience what you want in this area. What one joyful step could you take tomorrow to begin to follow this guidance?

2 | Get quiet and tune into your physical body. What inner guidance have you been receiving that might give you more energy or health? What one joyful step could you take tomorrow to begin to follow this guidance?

3 | Think about your relationships, including your relationship with yourself. Is there something that is not working as well as you would like it to? Picture the experience you would like. (Note: You cannot change another person, only yourself. Often when you change something about yourself—your attitude, perspective, actions—the other person changes their response to you). What about yourself could you change that would improve this situation? Stop for a moment and let ideas come to mind about what you might do to improve your experience of this relationship. Be willing to take action on your ideas.

CHAPTER 9

Coming Out of Survival

If you are experiencing an ebb, with more money going out than is coming in, don't panic. Do not lose confidence in yourself or think that somehow you have failed. The challenge of an ebb state is to believe in your future prosperity. Everything on earth is cyclical, and all phases are temporary. For every ebb there is a flow that will follow.

If you have a short- or long-term drop in your income, remember that it will be temporary, and focus on what you are learning from this experience. It is a rare company that does not go through ups and downs in the flow of sales created by natural business cycles. As you reach higher and higher levels of mastery with manifesting, you will be able to draw to you what you need when you need it, and you will be less affected by these natural cycles.

Use ebb periods to get even clearer about money in your life. Continue to magnetize and ask yourself, "What is the advantage in this situation?" There is always a higher reason for changes in the flow. Since you may have more free time during this cycle, use it to start doing those things you have been wanting to do: acquire new knowledge, think, relax, explore new avenues, or take that long-awaited vacation. You might want to look at new directions your work might take and explore new ideas that are emerging. There is always a way out of an ebb. There are ideas in your mind just waiting to be explored and tried out; pay attention to the beckoning whispers of the things you love to do as well as your dreams and visions.

The universe works in perfect ways.
It always serves my higher good.

The more you can appreciate the gifts you are receiving while the tide is out, the more rapidly the tide will come back in. Focus on the abundance you have rather than all the bills. See what new soul qualities you are developing, such as patience, trust, and love. Remember, you create what you focus on, and down cycles are always followed by up cycles. Think of a time in the past when you went through a hard time with money. See the strength it developed in you and how your life changed afterward. When you look at the past you can see how much progress and forward movement you have made after every ebb.

Sometimes you need to spend money before you earn it, as most businesses do. If you are spending money on things that will bring you future prosperity, see this as a demonstration of trust in your future earning ability. Do, however, be honest with yourself in your evaluation of what you need and how much future income you might expect. Evaluate your skills, knowledge, and the market, and make your decisions accordingly. For instance, new businesses sometimes get fancy offices and lots of equipment, hire staffs, and then find that they don't have the business to support these expenses.

$\text{M}y$ *debts represent my and others' belief in my future earning ability.*

If you are considering going into debt, check in with your inner guidance first and ask if it is appropriate. Incurring debt to finance a major leap forward has within it the possibility of bringing you more money than you borrow. Incurring debt to meet monthly expenses might indicate a basic problem in your financial setup. You can borrow money for rent, but rent is still going to be due next month. It is usually better to think about ways other than borrowing to create money on an ongoing basis.

Sometimes it seems necessary to borrow to make ends meet, to buy things you need, or to finance a new venture. If you have gone into debt, don't let the fact that you have debts keep you from feeling prosperous. If your debts seem unmanageable, if you feel you have borrowed beyond your ability to pay, go back to your original belief that you would be able to pay these debts off easily. You trusted yourself to have future income when you borrowed money; keep renewing that trust. Rather than worrying about your debts, pay gladly even a little payment each month. Visualize the amounts becoming less, and the debts will eventually be paid off.

Worrying about debts is non-productive. You may prefer not to be in debt, but you are not going to get out of debt unless you put your mind to creative ideas and work instead of worry. If you cannot make a payment, remember to keep in touch with your creditors. Tell them of your intention to pay, and send as much money as you can, even if it is only a portion of the payment that is due. Creditors are delighted to hear from you, and usually will accept whatever you can afford to pay if you make payments on a regular basis.

One family fell way behind in their monthly bills when the husband was laid off work. Creditors were calling them, and the wife was afraid to answer the phone or the doorbell because people kept showing up asking for their money. The situation looked very grim. One day someone told her that if you contact creditors and explain your situation, they usually make allowances.

She didn't think this would apply to her, since most of their creditors were big institutions. However, she bravely picked up the phone and called each creditor, explaining their misfortune and their intent to pay off the bills. To her amazement, every creditor was friendly and reasonable. She offered to pay each one $5 or $10 each month until she could resume larger payments, and each one accepted.

If you are in debt and you want to get out of debt, start by figuring out the total amount you owe. Then, forgive yourself if you have had any bad feelings about this debt, and realize that you borrowed because you and those you borrowed from believed in your future earning capacity. Picture your debt being totally paid off. Imagine the account reading: "$0.00 due. Paid in full." See yourself making the last payment; make the scene as real as possible. Experience the good feelings you will have.

Don't worry about how long it might take to pay a debt off; it will occur faster than you think. When you get ready to pay the next installment on your debt, first write out a "pretend" check for the full amount. Put this check where you will see it whenever you refer to the bill. As you pay the bill, send love and a mental thank-you to your creditor for his or her trust in you.

Many people determine their net worth by looking at the balance on their bank accounts. Even if you do not have a savings account and you have debts, you still have net worth— all your skills, knowledge, attitudes, education, experience, and contacts. Everything you have learned and every skill you possess are sources of future income. The skills and experience of your past are your net worth, and you can turn them into money.

My value and worth are increased by everything I do.

When you receive payment for work, you are exchanging your experience for money. Every day you are gaining experiences that can be turned into money; your earning power is growing. Your knowledge, skills, and experiences are worth money when used in the right way. In the future you will have even more skills that can create money for you. Even if you are in debt, you may still have a large net worth; it just hasn't yet been converted into dollars. If you are a student who went into debt to finance your schooling, you are creating a net worth of skills that will later be converted into money. Keep growing, expanding, and following your path, and your worth will continue to grow. As you grow, you will be able to earn more in the future to pay off past debts.

When you are living at a survival level, barely able to pay your bills, do not feel that you are a failure. This is simply the way you have chosen to learn many important lessons and experience the essence of who you are. You may be growing rapidly from this experience. You may be learning that you deserve to have abundance by experiencing the lack of what you want. Perhaps you are discovering how little it takes to live on, realizing you are not as dependent on having things as you thought. Perhaps you are learning that you can be generous even when you have very little. You might be learning the higher qualities of trust, compassion, and humility. You may be looking at what is important in your life, sorting through what is meaningful and essential to you and what is not. You might be learning how to let others give to you, or how to feel powerful without money. When you understand, embrace, and accept the lessons, you will no longer need this experience.

All *my experiences are opportunities to gain more power, clarity, and vision.*

Some of you are living on a survival level, putting most of your time and energy into paying your bills and meeting your basic needs. It is important to have enough money so that your energy can be put into your life's work and you are not in turmoil over lack of money. You may want to consider taking a temporary job as a stopgap measure that will help you pay your bills while you focus on finding your ideal job or career. At this stage, it is good to look around and find the easiest way possible, within the bounds of your integrity, to meet your basic needs. Even though a job doesn't use all your skills or isn't your idea of a perfect job, as long as the environment and activities of the business are satisfactory, it can help you build a foundation while you do other things.

Constant worry about money blocks your creativity and clear thinking. Getting yourself to a level where your bills are manageable and your basic needs are met will help you find and create your life's work more rapidly. Your soul does not care what job title you have. As long as you bring love and consciousness to your work, you will grow spiritually. If you decide to take a temporary job, do not think that you have sacrificed your ideals in some way. You may find that you are more effective in helping others if you are not struggling to survive yourself.

A temporary job may even have hidden surprises for you—a new friend or a skill that will help you later. Or, in some as yet unknown way, it may be a step toward your life's work. A temporary job will give you money, new skills, and possibly the opportunities you need to get a job that is more to your liking. Nothing is ever a wasted experience; even a routine job will teach you lessons you need to learn. Make sure this job doesn't take all your energy and time; you want to have enough left to activate your greater purpose.

Some of you may decide to stay at a survival level longer because you feel that taking a temporary job is a compromise. You may feel that doing anything other than your life's work is unacceptable, and that you are willing to live with less until your career is launched. Acknowledge that you are willingly deciding on this path. Do not let other people make you feel wrong about it. Just make sure that your basic needs are being met well enough so that you can spend the time necessary to launch your career.

Life is like a spiral. You will pass through every stage again and again, experiencing each stage from a higher and higher perspective. When you have very little money, you are learning many lessons that will make it easier to handle money when it comes. To break through this level, you may need to keep your life simple and uncomplicated in terms of money, expenses, demands, and needs. Think of yourself as the rose bush that is cut back in the winter so that it may grow strong in the spring. Use this time to get in touch with basic needs and eliminate those things that do not serve you.

When you don't know where the money will come from to pay your bills, or you are afraid to take the steps you are being shown from within that will help you change your current situation, you may be dealing with fear. Fear can be an easier feeling to change than you think. All it takes to release it is your willingness and intent to do so. One way to release your fears is by identifying specifically what you are afraid of. If you feel fear about your finances, use your imagination and ask, "What is the worst that can happen if I don't pay my bills this month?" Take each answer and again ask, "What is the worst that can happen?" Eventually you will come to your deepest fear. As you recognize it you can release it.

If the worst that can happen is that you might lose your job, have no money, and starve to death, deal with that fear first. When you identify your fears you can change them. Once you have dealt with the fear, you will see what actions are appropriate to take and be able to carry them out. As you face your fears, do not make them larger than they are. Once you see the worst that can happen, you will probably realize that you could handle it, and also that it is very unlikely that it will happen anyway.

For instance, one woman wanted to launch her own business but kept holding back; she knew she was afraid. She asked herself, "What is the worst that can happen if I start this business?" Her answer was, "Nobody will pay me. I'll have no business, then I won't be able to pay my bills." She kept asking, "What is the worst that could happen?" She replied, "If I can't pay my bills, I'll lose my home. My children won't eat. We'll starve." She again asked herself, "If that happens, what is the worst that could happen?" She thought, "I'll end up wishing I were dead."

Once she saw her fears she realized that there was very little chance that the very worst would happen, for she knew her brothers, sisters, and parents would at least bring her food. Bringing to the surface her worst fears also seemed to awaken her strength. For every part of you that is afraid there is also a part that knows you can succeed.

I *send love to my fears.*
My fears are the places within me
that await my love.

Take the same situation and imagine the very best that could happen. Every fear in you represents an area you are developing in this lifetime, a place within you that you are bringing to the light, changing negative energy into positive energy. Fears lose their power when you hold them up to the light of your consciousness. It is only when they lurk beneath the surface of your mind that they can cause you to avoid doing things that contribute to your higher path.

As you recognize each fear, you will be guided to ways of releasing it. One of the greatest gifts you can give yourself is to examine any recurring situation in your life that is causing you pain or struggle, and bring to light the fear that is behind it. Unlocking fear brings you tremendous gifts and opens up your greater potential, for each fear has buried within it many new pictures, insights, and revelations about who you are and who you can be. If you fear having enough money to do what you want, thoughts about world travel, a nice home, or financial independence will probably not come to your awareness. Releasing your fears will open up whole areas of growth and potential.

Another way to release a fear once you recognize it is to hold it up to the light of your soul. Imagine you are approaching a cool blue flame that represents your soul, and ask your soul to release, clear, and heal your fears. Release anything that is not for your higher good and ask it to release itself from you. You need only ask, and your soul will immediately begin to lead you to things that will help you release the fear. If you feel you are ready to let go of your fears, ask now for that release. Be open to creative new ways to get what you want.

You are not your fears but the self that experiences them. Instead of saying, "I am afraid," say "The feeling of fear is passing through me and I now easily let it go." Remind yourself that the part of you that feels the fearful feelings is only a small part of who you are.

You can learn to identify and connect with your strong self by sending love to your fearful thoughts and reassure them as you would a small, frightened child. Ask the fear if it has a message for you or if there is something it wants you to pay attention to. Once you love and release your fears, you will be able to move forward and claim the abundance that is your right much more rapidly.

I *speak of success and prosperity.* *My words uplift and inspire others.*

To increase your prosperity, talk about your abundance. Words are important. Everything you say has the potential to create the reality you experience. The universe responds to your positive talk. Even if you do not have something you want in your life right now, if you begin to talk and act as if you are certain you will have it, you will draw to you the circumstances to have it. Words affect your subconscious, which hears what you say and goes to work directly to make your words come true. The words, "I do not have enough money" go directly to your unconscious, which begins creating lack. Rather than saying, "I can't afford to buy this," say "I choose not to buy this at this time."

It is better not to speak of failure or financial disasters to others; if you do not have money right now, do not complain of your lack. Talk about your visions and your dreams. Speak of what is good in your life right now, and how positive you feel about the future. Speak to others of your confidence and trust in yourself, without emphasizing your lack. Your friends carry an image of you and when you think of yourself you pick up their pictures. If you speak to others of your prosperity, they will think of you as prosperous, they will carry positive mental pictures of you that you can tap into whenever you want. If you do not have money right now, speak as if you do.

I *live in an abundant world.* *All is perfect in my universe.*

If you feel right now that you do not have enough money, pretend that you have all the money you need and let the emotion of plenty come into your body. Your subconscious does not know the difference between what is really happening and what you imagine to be happening, so it goes out and happily creates your fantasy for you. Use the magnetism exercises in Chapter 4 and continue to magnetize what you have asked for, using the guidelines given. Create a vision of abundance and soon the world will reflect it back to you.

You may want to sit quietly and ask your wiser self to give you a message if there is anything you can do to increase your prosperity. If there is no message, assume what you have asked for is on its way to you and thank the universe and your higher self in advance for sending it. Continue your normal activities as if what you asked for were indeed coming. It will come whether you worry about it or not. Occupy yourself with other things to think about and do. You might want to check in now and then to see if there are any further whispers in your mind or messages that you might need to pay attention to. Handle them and then get back to whatever it is that appears to be the next thing to do in your life.

All you need to do is take one day at a time. Look at what actions you can take today to create money. Many of you get lost in the largeness of your visions and feel constant pressure from them. You may even feel like a failure because you have not accomplished your dreams. You do not need to feel that way. Simply concentrate on what you can do today. There is always something you can do right now to demonstrate your trust in your future. A feeling of powerlessness often comes from living the future, worrying about not having enough at some future time. You cannot change the future except by actions you take today, so focus on what you can do today to create prosperity.

Even the biggest plans are realized by living them one day at a time. In fact, the largest plans are often best created by looking at them day by day and month by month, constantly focusing on the next step. Creating your dreams takes patience, persistence, and commitment. Trust that whatever you are experiencing right now is perfect for your growth. Even if you have asked for abundance and you are experiencing what seems like the opposite, realize that experiencing its opposite can generate the energy you need to take a quantum leap forward.

COMING OUT OF SURVIVAL
PLAYSHEET

1 | If you are living at a survival level right now, ask yourself:

a. What am I learning by being in this situation?

b. In what ways am I growing stronger?

c. What qualities am I developing?

d. What have I discovered to be the truly important things in my life?

2 | If you are living at a survival level and feel like you are in a box with no way out, imagine the following:

a. Pretend you *are* in a box, or are looking at a wall that stands between you and having what you want.

b. What does the box look like? What is it made of? How thick is the wall?

c. Now, if you are imagining a box, build doors and windows in the box. Make as many doors and windows as you want until you feel free and comfortable. Or give yourself whatever tool is appropriate and tear down the wall until you are satisfied that you can easily and freely pass through to the other side. Working with symbols can create profound changes in your life. Each time you do this exercise those things represented by the box or the wall will begin to change, and new opportunities will come to you.

CHAPTER 10

*T*rusting

Trust is opening your heart, believing in yourself and in the abundance of the universe. It is knowing that the universe is loving, friendly, and supports your higher good. Trust is knowing that you are part of the process of creating, and believing in your ability to draw to you what you want.

*T*he universe is safe, abundant, and friendly.

Almost everyone goes through doubt about money—doubt that they will have enough, that the money they have will last, or that they have the ability to reach their goals. Even those who have gained great fortunes go through the same doubts, wondering if money will continue to come in or if what they have will last. Don't make yourself feel wrong for worrying about money. Do change the habit of worrying, or you will continue to worry about money no matter how much you have.

Many people think about money primarily when they perceive the amount of money they have as a problem. Doubt and worry about money have no relationship to the amount of money you have, nor is the amount of time you spend worrying about money related to how much money you can create. If you resolve to think about money only when you feel confident and peaceful, you can increase your magnetism to what you want.

If you are worrying about money, work on increasing your sense of well-being rather than thinking about money. Rather than asking, "How much money do I *need* today?" ask yourself, "How can I *create* money today?" There is an enormous difference in the energy you send out to the universe when you focus on creating money rather than needing money; the first is magnetic to money and the latter is not.

If you have taken whatever action seems appropriate, focus on other things, while still paying attention to any inner guidance about further actions. Ask, "What can I do right now that would increase my sense of well-being?" Take those actions that build up your good feelings, for they will invigorate you and change your state of mind to the point where you can think more positively about your finances. As you feel better, you will be more able to listen to your inner guidance and come up with new, creative ideas.

I *expect only the best to happen
and it does.*

Trust—expecting the best to happen, believing in your ability to create what you want, and knowing you deserve to have it—can be demonstrated in many ways. It is demonstrated by believing in something even when the outer world seems to reflect something else. It is demonstrated by talking of your abundance even if you do not yet see it around you.

It is not enough to sit around and believe. Demonstrate trust by listening to your inner guidance and taking action on it. Since you live in a world of form and substance, action is the physical link to having what you want. You can develop trust by putting your ideas into action, getting feedback, and seeing the results. Every time you are willing to take a risk you increase your ability to trust and believe in yourself. There is a difference between trust and hope. Trusting is believing and knowing that what you want will come; hoping is wanting something but not really believing that it will come.

Act as if you have the money for whatever you want. How many times have you held off getting something, thinking you didn't have the money, only to discover when you got it that you could have afforded it all along? If there is something you want, go out and look, visualize, and take action. You will often find it takes less money than you thought to get what you want, or a friend will have a used one to give you, or you will get it in an unexpected way. Take some action to demonstrate to the universe that you intend to have what you want. That action may not be the action that brings the object or the money directly to you, but your intent will signal the universe to begin bringing you what you want.

Suppose you want a new home, but you don't think you have enough money. Rather than give up, take action as if the money were already there. Start by imagining your ideal home or apartment. Go look at homes as if you have the money. Picture your perfect home over and over. Even though you do not have the money when you start, your intent to have your new home will create changes in what is possible. As your intent goes out to the universe, you become magnetic to certain people and events. You draw to you opportunities that wouldn't have existed if you weren't clear on your intent and taking action to bring it about.

One woman who did this was looking for an apartment in San Francisco. She was told that it was impossible to find even a studio for under $500 a month. She had only $250 a month to spend and wanted a place that had one bedroom, was within walking distance of her downtown office, and had a small deck or outdoor access for her cat. (Most places wouldn't even accept pets.) She didn't listen to her friends, who just shook their heads in disbelief. She had only two weeks to find a place, so she began to picture what she wanted clearly in her mind. She kept telling herself that it would be easy, and began to imagine the apartment and magnetize it to her.

One day, feeling the urge to take a walk, she came upon a woman sitting on the steps in front of a small building. For some unknown reason she felt drawn to tell the woman that she was looking for a place to live. It turned out that the woman was the landlord and had an apartment in the building that exactly fit her description. The landlord didn't need money from renting out the apartment, and because she had not liked her previous tenants, she had decided not to rent it ever again unless the right person came along. (It had been vacant for two years.) They got along well, and the woman agreed to let her move in, not even asking for first and last month's rent. She was able to have her cat, the rent was exactly $250 a month, and the building was within walking distance of her office.

Trust is the link between the mental world and the physical world. It provides continuity during the time that elapses between the conception of an idea and its manifestation. Realize that your dreams are already real on the mental plane; they are just awaiting the perfect time to appear in your physical reality. Trust your higher self to bring you the right things at the right time.

I *trust my ever-increasing ability to create abundance.*

You know when you are on the right path; doors open, people appear, coincidences happen. When you are not on your path or pursuing your higher purpose it may seem as if you are walking through glue and nothing is working. When you are following your path and your energy is flowing, your life usually works easily and well. This doesn't mean that you won't come across any obstacles. Your challenge is to tell if obstacles mean you are to reexamine your path and perhaps find another, or if they are there to help you develop the qualities of persistence and patience. There are no easy answers. Knowing when to push ahead and when to find another course of action comes from experience and self-awareness.

One way to tell whether obstacles are just part of your growth or are telling you to find another path is to look at what you want to accomplish. If your goals feel joyful or you feel a sense of joy in moving through an obstacle, knowing that doing so will bring you what you want, it may be appropriate to go through it. Some people find obstacles challenging because overcoming them adds to their sense of accomplishment when they do get what they want.

If you keep focusing on what you want and take action as it appears appropriate, the obstacle will probably start dissolving. If moving through the obstacle seems like a great struggle, it is probably telling you that there is a better way to accomplish your goal. Often those circumstances you see as barriers lead you in another direction that turns out to be a better way to go. Obstacles can also be there to protect you, to keep you from taking action prematurely, or to get you to pay attention to something you may have missed. They also give you the opportunity to deal with all the issues that need to be handled before you can take the next step.

One woman wanted to find a new apartment because the woman who lived above her was very noisy. She spent three weeks looking with no results. She kept affirming that her perfect home was now in her life. She kept pushing through all the obstacles, even though they seemed to indicate that taking another path of action might be more suitable. Several weeks after she started looking, the neighbor above her unexpectedly moved away, and a very quiet person moved in. She hadn't needed to move after all. She realized that every attempt to find a new apartment had been blocked, and her determination to move through the obstacles simply kept her struggling. She also realized that she loved her current home, except for the noise, and hadn't wanted to move.

I *accept prosperity and abundance into my life.*

When you ask for something that is way beyond what you have now, such as an enormous increase in your prosperity, it may take a while to come so that you can be prepared to handle it. Think of yourself as vibrating at a certain rate. Think of the amount of money you have now as in harmony with that vibration. If you were to be suddenly handed an enormous sum of money without adequate preparation, the vibration of the money would be out of balance with your vibration. You have heard of those who win a lot of money and spend it all in just a few years, ending up where they were before financially. Others who win a lot of money make very few changes in their lives, and it is several years before they are comfortable handling large sums of money and feel ready to make major changes.

It is important to prepare to have larger and larger sums of money so that when more comes it will be in balance with the rest of your life. You can accelerate this process by "wearing" the energy of larger sums before you receive them and mentally adjusting your energy until larger sums feel comfortable.

There may be times when nothing seems to be happening on the outside, but you are going through much change on the inside to prepare for what you are asking for. Keep trusting your ability to draw to you what you want while you are waiting for money to come, and realize that everything that is happening to you is preparing you to have it and helping you change your vibration to match the vibration of abundance when it arrives.

I *trust that everything comes at the perfect time and in the perfect way.*

It takes time for the new to come, and many of you quit too soon. The bigger the goal, the larger the step, and the longer it may take to have what you want. This is because there are a certain number of steps to be taken and events that must occur to get from where you are now to where you want to be. You can work with energy to speed up the process as described in Step 6 in the *General Magnetizing* exercise on page 43. While you wait for something to come, affirm your trust, develop your courage, and learn to take the steps and actions you are guided to take.

It is also important for things to appear at the right time—when you are ready for them. If something you want comes too early, the situation may not yet be right for it to blossom into its full potential. If something comes too late, some of the opportunities needed for it to fully develop may have passed. It would be like a seed deciding to come up in the middle of winter; it would be too early for that plant, and the seedling might not be powerful enough to survive. If the seed waited until late summer to come up, it might not have time enough to fully develop before the fall and winter. Timing is very important, and your higher self will bring everything to you in its perfect time.

If you look back at one thing you wanted that you didn't get, you will probably realize that it was something that would not have assisted you at that time. Some of the things you want to create might stand in your way if they were created at inappropriate times or in the wrong forms. You might need to get rid of them later. The time and energy it takes to let go of them might distract you from your path.

Developing trust is important. Keep your goal in mind and work steadily toward it rather than expecting instant results. You may not always understand where your inner guid-ance is leading you, and some of the actions you feel guided to take may not lead you to the results you expect. Trust that your inner messages are leading you to your goals, even if you do not know how at the time. Trust that you will get what you have asked for if it is for your higher good, and that everything that is happening is helping bring it to you. Evaluate the results your efforts are producing not by the money they in-stantly bring, but by how much you love what you are doing and the value your activities contribute to your life. As you continue following your inner guidance and doing things that are meaningful to you, you will create your dreams.

Every event you experience on your journey to create more abundance is happening to help you develop qualities you need to attract and have money. Remember some of the times when you trusted; you may have been in much worse straits than you are now. Perhaps you truly did not know how you would meet your bills, and yet you trusted and got through. If you are trusting that money will come and it has not come, trust that what is happening is for your higher good, even if you can't understand why right now. Not having something may push you into new areas of growth.

You may be in the process of getting what you asked for, or you may have already received the essence of it. Every-thing you attract comes to teach you something and to contrib-ute to your aliveness and growth. You do not always need physical results to gain these realizations. You may learn the lessons just from imagining having something, and not need to create it in physical reality. If you haven't yet received what you are magnetizing, look again at the essence of what you want, and see if you haven't in some way already received it. Go back and review the real purpose of why you want to create it, and examine if that purpose has already been real-ized in some other way.

If there is something you want or need and it will truly serve your higher purpose, it will come to you. Don't make yourself wrong, thinking that you aren't trying hard enough or that you have some inherent deficiency in your ability to manifest. Realize instead that this is a loving universe, and the only things you ask for that don't come to you are the things that do not serve your higher good or that have forms that are not right for you at this time.

I *surrender to my higher good.*

One of the final acts of creating money is to let go and surrender to your higher good. It is time to let things happen in their own way and in their own time. Trust is knowing that there is a higher power within you that will assist you in bringing what you have asked for in the right way, at the right time. Surrender means not putting worry and fear into the process, but instead taking responsibility for the results, expecting that only the best will happen.

Detachment is also important. Detachment is a mental letting-go, just as surrender is an emotional letting-go. If you feel you can't live without something, that your well-being is dependent upon your having it, you actually repel what you desire. When there is no neediness attached to having what you want, you can create it much more easily. It has been said that you can't have something until you don't need it. This is not the same as not wanting it. Let go of what you have asked for completely. Trust that whatever comes will serve you and be for your highest good, even if you don't understand why at the moment.

The universe works in perfect ways. You can get in touch with the perfection of the universe and learn to trust that it is loving and teaching you what you need for growth and expansion. No matter what is happening in your life, every situation is teaching you what you need to learn to become more powerful. Everything that is happening is in some way helping you achieve your greatest potential, awaken your inner strength, and gain new levels of mastery. You can learn to identify what each situation is teaching you. As you recognize what you are learning, you will be able to move through situations more rapidly, with joy rather than struggle. This truly is a loving, generous, abundant, and caring universe, and you will always be given what serves you best.

PLAYSHEET

1 | In three minutes or less, list as many items as you can that you wanted, imagined, or fantasized about having that you received.

2 | For several of the items you listed, recall the level of trust you had that you would get them. Describe how this trust felt, how you felt as you waited for these things to come, or what you did that affirmed your trust that they would come.

3 | List as many items as you can that you want now. Which do you trust that you will create?

4 | Pick one thing from your list. What action could you take to demonstrate that you trust you will get it?

CHAPTER 11

Miracles

Miracles come from love, are created by love, and are magnetized to you through love. Think of a miracle you created for someone else. Perhaps you gave someone something very valuable to him or her that you knew he or she needed. Remember the sense of love you felt for that other person. The miracle came from the love within you and gave you love also. The other person had to be willing to receive your gift for there to be a completion of the energy. If he or she hadn't been able to receive, there would have been no miracle. You need to be open to receive before the universe can bring you miracles.

When you want to give or receive love and miracles, all you need do is intend to do so. Reach for the highest and biggest vision; create quality in your experiences. Each one of you is a bundle of loving energy, capable of creating anything you choose. Miracles come from your love. If you are willing to open your heart, to love yourself and others, life will always be a miracle. The degree to which you are open and loving is the degree to which miracles will come your way.

You may have seen the parents of a child with physical or mental problems produce miraculous results through their love for the child, overcoming handicaps that were supposedly not medically curable. Miracles happen when you are willing to receive and give love. A miracle is a demonstration from the universe and your soul of their love for you. If there is anything you want, use your mind to visualize it, and then open your heart.

I *demonstrate love with action every day.*

When you spend and give with love, you create even more ways for money to come to you. A state of love is a state of receptivity to the abundance of the universe. The more love you send out to the world, the more abundance and miracles you will receive in return. Every time you pay a bill or receive money, see it as a gift of love. Make every exchange of money an opportunity to radiate love to those around you.

Sometimes your mind stands in the way of miracles. The mind is good for planning, setting goals, and visualizing. To speed up the process and create miracles after you have magnetized something, open your heart. Trust and believe in yourself, love others, and demonstrate that love with action every day.

Give people as much love as you can. Be gentle and kind, speak loving words, extend forgiveness to those who haven't honored you, and hold loving thoughts about others and honor them in all you do. Do not judge or criticize. Instead, at every moment, find a new opportunity to love. Remember, it is easy to be loving when people around you are loving; the challenge is to be loving when those around you are not. As you treat others with love and compassion, you draw to yourself opportunities, money, people, miracles, and even more love. Love puts you in a higher flow and draws good things to you. As you open your heart in new areas, you become magnetic to increased good and abundance.

Miracles are unexpected occurrences that bring you far more than you expect. They are synchronistic events that usually occur when you let go of attachment and trust your inner guidance. Often they come because of a call to the deepest part of your being for help. Crisis frequently creates miracles, for it calls the deepest part of your soul into consciousness. Your soul is always looking over you, sending you love and guidance. As you get quiet and go inward, you connect to that part of you which has the answers. When you go inward, reach your soul, and ask for help, answers come and miracles happen. You want to learn how to go to the depth of your being without crisis. Miracles are the result of reaching inward to your soul.

If you want something, ask your soul to provide you with a demonstration of its faith in and love for you. Then, open to receive and be willing to recognize your request when it comes. Every time you accept love from others, every time you open to receive love from the universe, you set in motion the creation of miracles in your life.

I *am linked with the unlimited abundance of the universe.*

When you are not receiving money from your usual sources, ask for it from unusual ones. Let it come from other places in the world, from other people, from unexpected sources. When you look around you and do not see yourself receiving what you want, begin asking that all channels of money open to you. When you are determined to have something only through a certain source, you cut off all the other ways it can come to you.

Remember also that the circumstances of your life can change for the better overnight. It does not need to take time to change the circumstances surrounding your prosperity unless you believe it must take time. Perhaps you can remember a time when you were worried one day about money and something good happened the next day that took away your worries. If you are feeling depressed about money, remember that this is only a temporary situation and circumstances can change.

Think of all the times you can remember that you received money or something you wanted in a totally unexpected way that seemed like a miracle. The more you are willing to hold positive thoughts, to listen to and take action on your inner guidance, to trust and believe in yourself, and to commit to your higher purpose, the more miracles you will attract.

The greatest miracle is life itself. You are the miracle, and you can create anything you want, which is another great miracle. There are no barriers, no limits to what you can have. The only limit is what you can picture for yourself, ask for, and believe you can have.

Miracles *are love in action.*

MIRACLES
PLAYSHEET

1 | Write down all the times you can remember that you received money or something that was special to you as a miracle, with a feeling of divine intervention, or in a totally unexpected way.

2 | Is there a miracle you would like in your life right now? Are you open to receive it? Ask now for that miracle to come into your life.

Creating Your Life's Work

You Can Do What You Love

Discovering Your Life's Work

You Have What It Takes

Believing in Yourself

Trusting the Flow

Moving to Your Higher Path

CHAPTER 12

You Can Do What You Love

You are a special, unique person and you have a mean-ingful contribution to make to the world. Every person is born with a purpose. There is a reason you are here; you have a role to play that no one else on the planet could fill. The special contribution you came to make is your life's work. When you are doing that work, you are following your higher path, and your life will be filled with increasing joy, abundance, and well-being.

As I do what I love, money and abundance flow freely to me.

Finding your life's work allows you to create abun-dance and money easily. The job or activities that are meant to be your life's work involve doing what you love with your time and energy. When you love what you do you feel alive, happy, and fulfilled. You radiate joy and draw many good things to you. You can make money doing work that you don't like, but it will take more effort. Not liking what you do with your time and energy diminishes your flow of abundance; loving what you do brings abundance more easily and effortlessly.

Think of a gardener caring for his crops. The gardener who loves his crops will go out whenever necessary to weed, prune, and till the soil. He will protect his plants and oversee even the smallest detail. He will watch lovingly over each plant, doing everything he can to give it the opportunity it needs to grow strong and bear fruit. Of course his crops are more beautiful and more fruitful than those of a gardener who resents the work, tends his plants only when he has to, and puts minimum attention into gardening. Each will reap a harvest, but the gardener who loves his crops will have the larger harvest. He will also feel that growing his crops is fun and joyful, while the other gardener will feel that it takes much hard work and struggle to produce even a small harvest.

If you are already doing what you love for a living, you may want to go directly to the next section, *Having Money*, on page 193. If you want to get a better job, find more meaningful work, go to school, start your own business, create more enjoyable activities in your life, or look at ways to make your life's work more effective, you may want to read this section and complete the playsheets. They will show you how to use your energy to easily draw to you a job, career, or activities you enjoy. If you aren't interested in exploring your life's work at this time, you may want to simply work with the Exercise, *Energizing a Symbol of Your Life's Work*, on page 135, and then continue on to the next section, *Having Money*, on page 193. Energizing the symbol of your life's work will begin the process of drawing your ideal work to you whenever the time is right.

Activities you love involve using the skills and talents you will use in doing your life's work. This work can take many forms; one job may represent your life's work at one time in your life and other jobs may at other times. For example, one man's life's work was to inspire people and bring out the best in them. In his jobs as a waiter, busboy, clerk, and warehouseman he always cheerfully encouraged people and helped them discover their strengths. Later in life he started a writing career and wrote inspirational books that encouraged people to be all they could be and live joyful lives. Once his books were published, he became a popular public speaker, traveling around the country giving inspirational talks. He brought his highest skills of inspiring people to each job, although the forms of his jobs changed and evolved as he grew.

I *have a unique, special contribution to make.*

You will recognize when you are doing your life's work by the feelings of vitality and aliveness it gives you. You will feel that your life has greater meaning and that you are making a worthwhile contribution. You will have a compelling vision or goal. You will feel happier in every area of your life. Your work will allow you to express more fully who you are; it will help you grow and evolve.

You do not have to change jobs to do your life's work. You can make a meaningful contribution in any job you have, in whatever role you play, for in any job you can focus on how you are helping people; you can spread good feelings and touch everyone you contact with your inner light. You don't need to have a job or even be in business to be doing your life's work. You can express your life's work through community activities or hobbies. You may be raising a family as your life's work, helping to guide your children's life-force energy into a higher order. When your life is filled with meaningful activity, you radiate joy and love and are magnetic to abundance.

You can have fulfilling, satisfying work. You can feel alive every day of your life and make money in the process.

You can work in a supportive environment, around people you enjoy, doing what you love. As you use your special skills and talents, you can draw to you the opportunities to make money in ways that allow you full self-expression, ways that challenge and stimulate you. As you do what you love, you enrich the lives of the people around you and add more light to the world. In doing your life's work you are accomplishing what you came to earth to do.

Whatever you love to do will also help others in some way, for it is the nature of the universe that when you use your highest skills you automatically contribute to others. When you serve others, giving fully of your talent and skill to whatever you do, your work and services will be in demand and money will flow to you. Even if it doesn't appear that there will be more money in doing what you love, trust your heart and follow your higher path, for there will eventually be much more money and abundance from following this path than any other.

E*verything I do adds*
beauty, harmony, order, and light
to the universe.

Enlightenment comes from learning to put awareness and consciousness into all you do, bringing the energy around you into greater harmony, beauty, and order. Doing your life's work provides a vehicle for your enlightenment and spiritual growth, for when you love what you do you naturally put attention and awareness into your activities.

Your higher self speaks to you through your feelings, imagination, desires, and dreams. It shows you your life's work by guiding you to the things that are joyful and giving you pictures of what you love to do. Your life's work will be something you think about, feel connected to, are familiar with, or are already working on. It may be something you do in your free time for fun or something you tell yourself you would do if you had more free time or money. Your life's work will involve making a contribution to humanity, animals, plants, or the earth itself.

Your life's work is also indicated to you by your dreams and fantasies about your ideal life. You may dream of being out in nature, sailing around the world, writing a book, creating music or art, spending your time in training for a sports activity, raising a family, or teaching a class. You may want to run a business of your own or counsel people. Your deepest desires and dreams come from your soul. Your soul is not limited by the identity you have right now; it sees the larger picture of who you are and knows what is possible for you to accomplish in this lifetime. It shows you your potential and direction by giving you dreams of your ideal life. Don't discard your fantasies as merely wishful thinking. Honor them as messages from the deepest part of your being about what you can do and directions you can choose.

Your life's work may not yet exist as a job you can find. It may be a job you will create. Humanity is undergoing a shift in consciousness. New forms will be needed to put this higher consciousness into place. The old forms are going to change; thousands of people will be changing jobs and launching new careers. You are here right now to help build the new jobs and structures that will support this new consciousness. It is up to you to recognize the new opportunities, sense where the needs are, and create the forms that will fill them. As this new consciousness spreads, you will be feeling a stronger and stronger urge to do work that empowers you and others, challenges you to grow, and offers you a chance to put the energy around you into a higher order.

I *am in charge of my destiny.*
I am the builder of my life.

You may be feeling an inner urge to change what you are doing and find work that is more meaningful. Many of you have worked in jobs where you found little satisfaction. You may have gone from job to job, or stayed with one job for a long time but still felt like something was missing. You may have had to create your own jobs, even if you worked for an employer. You may have found that you were frequently making suggestions to your company on how things could work better, looking for ways to improve your job.

You may have been hearing whispers that tell you it is time to consider new things. You may have found yourself thinking, "I wish I had a better job" or "I wish my work were more meaningful." A job you previously enjoyed may now be routine or something you do because you need the money, not because you love it. What was once easy may have become difficult or boring. If you are hearing any of these inner messages, it is time to start examining your path.

To create your life's work, do not feel you have to or should do something other than what you are doing. Forcing or pushing yourself usually results in resistance, not forward movement. You don't need to totally change your life; you can create your life's work gradually, one step at a time. What you are doing right now contains the seeds of your life's work. What you are seeking is to express your special skills more frequently and to use them in a way that provides you with a livelihood now or in the future. As you do more and more of what you love, you will create abundance in its highest form— a life that is fulfilling, alive, happy, and full of love.

D*o what you love*
and money will come.

Energizing a Symbol of Your Life's Work

You can draw your life's work to you by making a symbol for it and energizing the symbol. Symbols are very powerful because they bypass all your thoughts and belief systems and represent the pure energy of your soul.

Preparation:

Find a time and place where you can relax and think without interruption for a few minutes. Relax and prepare yourself in the same way as in the *Learning to Relax* exercise on page 14.

Steps:

1. Find a time when you can be alone. Close your eyes and sit quietly for a moment. Ask your soul or higher self to show you a symbol that represents your path of most light, your life's work. Take whatever picture comes to your mind, for it will be the perfect symbol to energize at this time. Imagine that you are holding this symbol in your hands. Picture energy coming from your soul and going directly into your symbol, energizing it. Then imagine that you are placing this symbol on top of a mountain. Visualize a path leading from you to your symbol at the top of the mountain. See yourself walking or dancing joyfully up this path, your whole being focused on reaching the top of the mountain.

2. When you reach the top, congratulate yourself on your single-minded dedication to your purpose, and for how easily you reached your goal. Let yourself feel the feelings you will have when everything in your life is working, when your environment is totally nurturing, alive, and utilizing your highest potential. Take your symbol in your hands and bring it into your heart, letting it energize and radiate light throughout your body, until every cell is aligned with your higher purpose

and life's work. Then release this symbol to the higher forces of the universe. This energizes your symbol.

3. As you work with your symbol, you will draw to you specific ideas of what you can do to accomplish your life's work. Doing this exercise will draw to you the circumstances, people, and events that will launch you on your path. Your intent is important, as is your commitment. The stronger your intent and the more you believe that your life's work exists, the more you will experience success as you listen to and take action on your inner guidance.

CHAPTER 13

Discovering Your Life's Work

One way to discover your life's work is to observe what you love to do and what you do naturally, noticing which skills you enjoy using. Your life's work will involve using those skills. Once you have identified them, you can concentrate on using them more, and draw opportunities to you to make money and support yourself through them. You can also find ways to use those skills in other areas of your life, turning all your activities into expressions of your life's work.

Everything you enjoy doing—every job, hobby, and activity—involves using certain skills. You can discover what those skills are by asking yourself questions. What things do you love doing in your job? What are your hobbies? What community activities do you do because you love them? What daily activities bring you joy and aliveness? Are you interested in singing, dancing, or the arts? Are you interested in writing, channeling, counseling, or bodywork? What do you enjoy most? Healing, helping, teaching, or empowering others? Negotiating, managing, organizing, leading, networking, and so on? Are you drawn to business skills, money management, art production, or scientific or research skills? Do you want to develop creativity, imagination, or your abilities to observe and draw conclusions? Do you want to work with things such as equipment, computers, and machines, or information such as numbers, statistics, or research results? Do you want room to be creative, or do you prefer work that is straightforward and logical? Do you like to work with your hands or voice? Do you enjoy communicating with people in person or on the phone? Get quiet for a moment and ask for some ideas about the skills you love to use and the talents you express naturally.

For instance, one woman found that she was spending all her free time cutting her friends' hair and helping them improve their personal appearance. She loved working with her hands and being around people. One day it occurred to her that her life's work was to help other people feel good about themselves by working with their appearance. She went to beauty school at night while she continued her job. She was eventually able to quit her job and open her own successful hair salon.

I *honor and use my special skills and abilities.*

Perhaps one of your highest skills is counseling people. You may have a knack for assisting people in finding solutions to their problems and creating new visions for themselves. You can find ways to use these skills in any job you have, and thus do your life's work more fully right now. Or, these skills may lead to some form of counseling as your full-time profession. The more opportunity you have to do activities you love, the more you will make the contribution you came to make and the more abundance you will attract.

One woman loved dogs, and her skill in handling them made her home a favorite boarding place for many of her friends' dogs when they went away. She recognized that using her skill of relating to dogs was more joyful than using any of her other skills, so she went into business grooming and boarding dogs. She realized that another talent she had was helping people relate better to their pets, and she found many opportunities to do so. Because she loved her work so much and used her higher gifts, she brought much light into people's lives and the lives of their pets, and made a very good living as well.

What you are doing right now has within it the seeds of your life's work. As you may have discovered, each time you get a new job you use many of the skills you have already developed. It is as if every job prepares you in some way for the next one. Every skill you acquire that you love using will be important as you follow your higher path. You may not understand why you took a job or developed a particular talent or ability, but the skills you have learned will be of value to you. Trust that what you are doing now is helping you gain skills that will be used in your greater life's work.

For instance, Duane found that his career in geology, while seemingly quite different in form from his path of healing people, involved using many of the same skills. As a geologist he loved his frequent flying trips, observing the earth and mapping out earthquake fault lines. This involved visually recognizing and interpreting detailed earth patterns and sorting out important from unimportant data. It was a skill that took quite a bit of practice to develop. Interestingly, the essence of the skill turned out to be very similar to his ability to look at people's energy patterns clairvoyantly, which also required visually recognizing and interpreting detailed patterns and being able to distinguish the important data from the unimportant data.

You are learning skills right now that you may use later in different ways. Sanaya used to love spending hours crocheting and doing needlework. She realized later that these hobbies developed her ability to quiet her mind and achieve a state of relaxation and meditation. She now uses these skills in her channeling.

I find my life's work by looking within rather than without.

Do not try to figure out what to do with your life by looking at the world and asking "What can I do for the world?" Look at yourself and ask, "What do I want to do that I love to do? What attracts me? What excites me? What are the issues I am working on in my life? What can I get enthusiastic about doing?"

One man wanted to open a retail store, although he did not have any previous experience. He chose the type of store to open by looking at what kinds of stores were doing well, rather than at what products he was interested in selling. He chose to open an ice cream store, even though he had very little experience with or interest in ice cream. The business was not joyful for him to run and he didn't draw many customers. The store barely broke even, even though he worked long hours. He finally asked for inner guidance about how to improve his business, and got the message that he needed to sell products he was interested in.

He began to look at his life, observing what he was interested in and familiar with. He realized that he loved running, and that sports had always fascinated him. He remembered how much trouble he had in finding running shoes and other supplies, having to go to many stores to find what he wanted. He decided that he would love to open a store specializing in runners' shoes and supplies, which he did after selling his ice cream store. He had no idea that a boom in jogging was just beginning. His store was very successful and he loved his work.

I have a wealth of valuable skills and talents.

You have many skills and talents and an amazing wealth of past experiences and knowledge. You can identify some of your skills and knowledge by looking at all the schools, workshops, and classes you have attended. Look at the books you have read, the tapes you have listened to, and the educational television programs you have watched. When you evaluate your skills, remember all the jobs you have had, even volunteer jobs, such as helping out at your children's school or at your church, as well as all the activities you did after school and during the summer.

Do you love organizing and running a household, working on a committee, fundraising, or coordinating a group of people and scheduling their time? Look at your hobbies. Do you belong to clubs such as bridge or sports clubs? Do you love the theater, opera, ballet, or symphony? Do you love arts and crafts? Do you enjoy building things, writing poems, or telling stories? You have a rich and varied background of skills, probably more than you have ever taken note of.

After looking at the skills you want to use, look at your dreams. The more detail and clarity you can bring to your dreams, the more you will be able to attract what you want. As you examine your dreams of your ideal life, the things you are drawn to, and the environment and kinds of people you want to be around, you are identifying the elements of your life's work. Your dreams act as a mental model—much like an architect's blueprints—that helps your higher self go out and bring your higher path to you.

I *now have my ideal life.*

Your fantasies about your ideal life may not appear to be practical or profitable. They may seem very large and far away, and you may see no way to make them come true. It may seem that you need to have a lot of money before you could carry them out. You may think that you need to work at something you don't love while you save money to eventually do what you love to do. Some people say, "I will work in this job until I have the money to do what I want." They often do not get the money they think is needed, and instead spend their lives working at jobs they don't enjoy.

Go directly to what you want. You will be much better off doing what you love, for money will come through that also, and usually in far greater amounts. If you want to travel around the world, start with a job that facilitates traveling, such as working for an airline or a travel agency. You will feel more alive and fulfilled and thus be more magnetic to abundance. What is your dream? Take a moment to get in touch with it.

What environment have you dreamed of working in? You may have pictured working outdoors, with nature and animals. Or you may prefer to work indoors, with people or equipment. Decide where in the country you want to work, and whether you thrive better in a city or a rural environment. Do you want to work in an office, drive a truck, be on a construction site, on a boat, on a plane, in one place, or in many places? What would your work environment look like? Think about what type of people you want to be around and the relationships you want with these people. You may want to be their employer, co-worker, or employee. You may enjoy being with younger and older people, people your own age, many people, few people, or you may prefer working alone.

Have you dreamed of working in areas such as medicine, nutrition, sports, politics, science, or education? Your dreams are giving you clues about where you might discover your life's work. Pay attention to the issues that arouse your concern, such as planetary peace, animal rights, environmental issues, the homeless, foreign affairs, space exploration, and so on. You can design into your work just the right amount of physical, mental, and emotional challenge. Do you like a physically active job? Do you thrive on a busy, active day or do you like a quiet, peaceful pace? Be specific and clear about what you want, because you will get it.

One woman found a picture in a magazine of what her perfect office would look like, down to the plants, artwork, and unusual blue typewriter on the desk. She put the picture on her wall and kept visualizing an office environment like the one in the magazine. Several years later she quit her job and went on a job interview. To her amazement, she walked into an office that looked just like the picture, except that it had a yellow typewriter. She got the job, and when she sat at her desk, they told her they had ordered a new typewriter for her—a blue one. Unfortunately, she had forgotten to picture the type of people she wanted to work with, the level of responsibility, opportunities for advancement, and many other details. She quit the job several months later because it didn't suit her deeper needs.

*I know what I love to do
and I do it.*

Be clear about the type of office situation you would like. Some of you do best working for a company, receiving a regular paycheck or commissions, and some of you love to run your own business. You may love working for a large company or prefer a small one. You can have anything you want; all you need to do is decide what it is you want.

If you have had past work experiences, reflect on whether you work well with co-workers and enjoy working as part of a team or prefer to run things by yourself. Some of you like to share risks, and some of you like to make all the important decisions on your own. Decide if you want to work for one employer or do contract work for several employers.

What monthly income do you dream about? What level of responsibility do you want? You may dream of working for a large organization and being given larger and larger leadership responsibilities. Think about the level of security you want in a job, the status, and the opportunities for advancement. If you thrive on recognition, include that in your dream. If you want a lot of autonomy and freedom, ask for that as well. Ask yourself if you thrive on a well-defined, structured job or if you want constant change and variety.

I *allow myself to think and dream in unlimited ways.*

What would you do with your days if you could do anything you wanted? What would a period of several months in your ideal life be like? Would you work three or four days a week at one task and do something else the other days? Would you work on a variety of projects, or would you focus on one undertaking? Would you work intensely for one month and take the next month to do something different? Take the time to daydream and fantasize about your ideal life.

Don't put any restrictions on your dreams. If you catch yourself saying, "That would be nice, but it's too much to ask for," stop. Ask for it anyway! This is a time to engage in unlimited thinking. Don't feel you have to create your dreams instantly; the first step to creating them is just putting the pictures in your mind. Your thoughts are real. As you get specific about what you would like, your higher self immediately goes out and begins to create it for you. You do not have to know when or how it will come. All you need do is get clear about what you want, and dare to think big.

One man decided to look closely at what his dream of an ideal job would be. He wrote out all that he wanted from a job. He loved listening to and reading the news, so he decided that his perfect job would allow him to be home watching television and reading news journals. He was a gambler at heart and loved to play games like bridge for money, so he decided his perfect job would have elements of risk and high stakes to it. He also loved statistics, his major in college. He wanted to work alone, have the potential to make a large amount of money, and work only part of the day. He loved getting up early and having afternoons free to play tennis and other sports. He didn't want to have any employees or work for someone else. Although he didn't believe it would be possible to find a job that offered all of his wishes, he wrote them down anyway and decided to let his higher self find a job that met all of his wishes.

Shortly thereafter, he made a new friend who was dealing in gold futures and other commodities. He was instantly fascinated and began spending all his free time studying the market. He loved charting commodity prices and had graphs all over his walls on which he plotted potential price fluctuations. He spent hours studying a theory that calculated and predicted commodity prices by tracking statistics of cycles and wave patterns. He also found that watching television and reading news journals was an important part of his research.

He became so accurate at predicting what would happen in the commodity market based on his charts and graphs that he started making money. The broker he traded with began asking him for advice that he passed on to other clients. Eventually the broker asked him if he would trade for some of his other clients, which he did. A while later he was able to quit his job and work at trading full time. This allowed him to work mornings and take afternoons off. He didn't need any employees and was able to work at home. He loved the element of risk and the high stakes, and the job required him to use his knowledge of statistics.

Ask for what you want, no matter how impractical or farfetched it may seem. Your higher self will go out and begin bringing your wishes to you. As you allow yourself to dream, you are creating a new reality.

DISCOVERING YOUR LIFE'S WORK
PLAYSHEET

Imagine you are living a life that is truly joyful and loving. How would you answer the following questions: (Remember, this is your joyful fantasy life. Use your imagination.)

1 | What activities are you doing or what type of skills are you using, such as reading, talking, negotiating, counseling, thinking, writing, organizing, or managing; working with children, running or sports, working with objects, building things, or fixing machines or equipment; or working with plants, animals, or data? List at least five, preferably more.

2 | How many hours a week do you devote to moneymaking activities? What hours do you work? How many days in a row do you work each week or each month?

3 | Do you have a physically active, fast-paced job or do you work in a slow, relaxed atmosphere?

4 | Do you work with the same people every day? What are these people like? What role do you play with them? How much of the time do you work alone?

5 | What does your work environment look like? Is it indoors or outdoors, in your home, or in a center or office? Do you travel? If so, where and how often? Do you work in the city or the country?

6 | What status do you have or what role do you play? What responsibilities do you have? What opportunities for advancement? Are you part of a team? Do you work for a large or small company, or for yourself? Do you work for one employer or group, or do you contract your work to several clients?

As you imagine this joyful life in more and more detail, continue refining and adding to your answers, thinking of even more possibilities and choices and imagining yourself having even more than you did the previous time. You may find that you get clearer about what you want as you focus on it and take away any limits you have placed on what is possible. You are creating a model that tells your higher self what your ideal life would be like. As you complete these questions, your higher self is already beginning to find ways to bring your ideal life to you. Are you ready to have it?

CHAPTER 14

You H*ave*
W*hat* I*t* T*akes*

You can draw your life's work to you more quickly by developing the inner strengths and resources you will need to successfully carry it out. You do not need to take large risks or big steps that are inappropriate for you. By starting with small steps and developing your inner resources, each move you make will be an easy next step. As you take small steps, you will discover that your dreams are within your reach and easier to accomplish than you imagine.

A*ll answers are within me.*
I follow my inner wisdom.

Doing your life's work will require the skills of listening to and following your own wisdom. It will require making yourself rather than anyone else the authority on what is good for you. Creating your life's work is a process of discovering yourself. You do so by going within, rather than looking for answers outside yourself. Many of you think that others have the answers, particularly in areas you are unfamiliar with. There is a time when it is appropriate to listen to outside authorities, such as when you are new to something and need to acquire knowledge about it. But after you have gathered other people's wisdom and knowledge, it is best to rely on your own wisdom in making decisions. You may think that others know better than you what direction your career needs to take, what investments to make, or what would work for you, but you are the best authority on how to live your life.

To create your life's work you will need to learn to solve your own problems, which you might instead call your "challenges" or "opportunities for growth." While it is fine to seek outside guidance, make the final decisions from your heart and follow your intuition. As you do your life's work, you will be creating your own path from day to day. No one is going to structure it or lay out a blueprint for you. You will have a sense of control over your life and know that you are in charge of your destiny. As you commit to your life's work, you commit to being the builder of your own life. You can design your future by being alert and aware of opportunities, knowing when to take action and when not to. You can start to do this in small ways now.

No matter what you are doing, take time to think about your life and look for creative ways to solve some of your problems. Discover your own answers. As you develop the skill of creative thinking, you will be able to find more effective ways to do your work and be more successful. You can begin to develop the skill of creative thinking by working with some of your simple problems, such as how to cut down on your cooking time if it is taking time you would rather spend on other activities. You could decide to cook larger quantities and freeze what you don't need immediately for future meals.

As you think about how to increase the harmony and flow in your life in small ways, you are developing the skill of creative problem solving. When you encounter challenges on your path, you will already have the skills you need to handle them creatively and to find solutions. Become resourceful; rather than enduring bad situations, look for ways to make them better.

I *am a valuable person.*
My path is important.

Some of you have difficulty accomplishing your life's work because you are too busy supporting others in their careers or life's work. You may be setting aside your own work until the person you are helping succeeds. Helping others get their work out to the world and being part of a team can be very important. You will know if this role is your life's work because serving in this way will be joyful and feel good deep within you. If you are helping others out of obligation, not out of joy, check again to see if this is truly what you want to do.

Some of you are supporting others because you feel your path, ideas, or creativity are not important enough to develop. Your life's work is as valuable as anyone else's, even if it doesn't seem as significant. Even though other people appear to have more glamorous jobs, make more money, or reach larger audiences, it does not make their path any more important, or any less important, than yours. What you are here to do is as important a contribution as anyone else's, be it to raise your children in the best way you can, make a contribution through the job you have, or heal and help others.

Take a moment right now to ask that part of you that is so good at helping others if it would be willing to commit its energies to helping you discover and carry out your own life's work. It is usually delighted to be asked to help you.

I *value my time and energy.*

Some of you need to develop the skill of honoring your time and energy. You may be a natural counselor, teacher, and healer, and end up spending more time than you want helping your friends or family solve their problems. They may keep you busy for hours on the phone or in person as they seek out your love and reassurance. You may be tempted to jump in and show them what to do, or even do it for them. It is fine to spend your time taking care of others if it is truly joyful, for doing this may be your life's work. However, many of you put your time into helping others out of obligation, not joy. You may feel you are being selfish putting time and energy into your own life. Your path is important, and it can unfold only if you put time and energy into it.

Think of friends you are pouring a lot of energy into. Are they truly growing and using your help, or are they staying the same? Do you feel drained after helping them, or recharged? If you feel drained, if they haven't made any real changes in their lives, they aren't using your help to grow. If you are spending all of your time advising and counseling your friends, it may be that your life's work is to counsel people. You may want to explore ways you could help people as part of your profession. When you do, you will be connecting with people who come to you because they are ready to grow. You will be recharged by helping them, and your assistance will make a real difference in their lives.

My path and life's work are my highest priorities.

A lot of you end up doing so many small tasks that you don't have time to create your life's work; you confuse busyness with accomplishing your higher purpose. You may have stacks of chores to be done and be rushing around, busy every moment. If you are going to get to your life's work, you need to take time to start it. Some of you say, "I'll do the important things after I finish all these errands, housework, paperwork, and so on." By the end of the day you may be too tired or have no time left.

Do those activities that take you closer to your life's work the first thing each day, or as soon as you possibly can. Spend five minutes thinking about your higher path as you wake up. Ask yourself, "Is there one action I could take today that would bring my life's work closer?" or "What is the most important action I could take today?" Make that your priority; do it before you do other things. It may be something as simple as energizing the symbol of your life's work, making a phone call, getting a book about a topic you are interested in, or setting up a space in your house to do a certain activity. You will be amazed at the way your life will change if the first thing you focus on and accomplish every day is something that will help make your dreams come true.

One very important principle in creating your life's work is right timing. You may have heard the expression, "an idea whose time has come." Begin now to affirm that you will be in the right place at the right time. Keep that thought in mind, and trust that your feelings of joy or resistance are helping you create this as a truth.

For instance, one woman was struggling to write a book. She would force herself to write for an hour or two each day. The ideas just wouldn't come, and finally she quit trying. Two years went by, during which she made sporadic attempts to write, but was never able to stay with it steadily. She kept blaming herself, telling herself she was a failure, and that she just didn't have the discipline necessary to write.

Her work brought her into contact with many sick people, and she began working with them, teaching them the spiritual principles she knew. Many started to get better, or find the inner peace they had been seeking. More and more people started coming to her, and she decided to give classes. She tape-recorded her talks, and since there was so much demand for her teachings, she transcribed the tapes, bound the transcriptions, and gave them to her students to use as a study guide. They began to share them with others, and she found herself constantly making more copies to meet the increasing demand.

One day, an editor for a large book publishing company called her. A friend had given the editor her manuscript and the editor wanted to publish it. It turned out that the topic was very "hot" at that time, and her book sold quite well. She realized in looking back at her earlier attempts to write that she needed to grow and learn a lot before her book could be written. She also saw that the timing had not been right; if she had somehow managed to have her earlier book published it wouldn't have been as successful.

If you are working on a project, remember that your higher guidance is always helping you get it done at the right time. If, no matter what you do, you keep resisting or struggling with it, it is either the wrong project or the wrong time. You may need to do something else first and then come back to it. Put your energies elsewhere and follow your joy.

You may have been thinking for months about making a change, but not know what to do, or feel that you don't have the option of leaving your current situation. Or you may know what you'd like to do but feel it will cost too much money or require you to do something beyond your skills and resources. Be loving to yourself if you haven't taken action yet. Remember, there is a period of inner work before changes take place. You may be changing your thoughts, reevaluating your life, observing things from a new perspective, and gathering the energy needed to make a change. The greater the outer changes you want to make, the greater the inner changes that must be made first.

I *accept and love myself for who I am right now.*

Learn to love and accept yourself for who you are right now. Love all the things you have already created. You do not need to be perfect before you do your life's work; accomplishing your life's work will help you grow and evolve. As you love and accept who you are right now, you make it possible to move in new directions. You have been doing the best you know how. Start appreciating yourself for who you are rather than thinking about who you wish you were. This will help you move forward more easily. Is there anything you have been criticizing yourself for lately? If so, for one day, every time you think of this thing see if you can thank yourself for all the good things you are doing instead.

Many of you have an inner sense that you have much to accomplish in this lifetime, as if you have a "mission." You may worry if you haven't yet found out what it is. Trust that everything you are doing is laying the foundation for your greater work to unfold. Some people's life's work is accomplished at an early age. Some people's life's work requires years of gaining knowledge and experience before it can be accomplished, and they do their most important work in their later years. If you have that inner sense that you came to do important work and you haven't yet discovered the form of that work, keep following your inner guidance and make choices that bring you joy, as they are leading you to the greater contribution you came to make.

Rather than being hard on yourself for not having accomplished more, spend a moment congratulating yourself on how far you have come and how much you have already accomplished. Give yourself reasons why it may be perfect to be where you are today, rather than criticizing yourself because you haven't done more. Focus on all you are doing and learning that is preparing you to have more. Acquiring the skill of talking positively to yourself will help you develop inner strength and trust to take the actions you will need to take as you follow your path.

Take the time to find and do the things you enjoy. Start by picking something small you love to do, such as baking cookies for your children, and do it more frequently. One woman who loved baking cookies now has a large and successful chain of cookie stores. A woman who loved arranging dinner parties eventually started her own business planning dinner parties for busy business executives. A man who enjoyed building things in his workshop started a very successful business making one-of-a-kind furniture pieces.

If you want to turn the activities you love into a potential livelihood, you can begin now to connect doing them with making money by charging for your services. When you charge money for doing something you love to do, you link having abundance with using your special gifts. It is a wonderful message to your conscious mind that your time, energy, and skills are valuable. Some of you accept money only for doing jobs you don't like, and feel guilty asking for money for your special talents and services. When you do this, you are telling yourself that making money is a function of doing what you don't like, and that it is not possible to make a living doing what you enjoy. Although when you first start you may not want to charge money while you gain experience, you will need to charge money eventually for these talents and skills if you want to launch a career using them. If you do not charge for them, you will have less time to use your special gifts (unless you have an independent means of support) and thus less time to make the contribution you came here to make. Even if you begin by charging just a little, it is a positive message to yourself that you are now associating the activities of your life's work with abundance.

Don't worry in the beginning if your skills don't earn you enough to live on, if you charge less than others doing similar things while you acquire more skills, or if you give more than you receive. You don't have to support yourself from the income or make a lot of money at first. Just putting into action your new belief that you can make money for doing what you love is a fair exchange for you. There will come a time when you can bring what you charge into line with what your services are worth and what you need to support yourself. As you gain experience and learn to honor what you do, you will find others honoring your increased worth as well.

Observe where you are spending your time and what you do naturally. One man, recently out of college, was feeling pressure from his parents to go to work, so he got an office job. He wanted to discover his life's work, and knew it wasn't working in an office. He began to examine where he was putting his time and energy, and realized that after work he couldn't wait to get to his exercise classes. He decided to become an exercise physiologist, designing exercises both as therapy for people with physical problems and to help people get fit. He enrolled in school and reduced his job to part-time. He is still in school and feels more alive than ever. Even the part-time job has become fun again, because he knows it is paying his school tuition. Follow your interests; for what you are enthusiastic about is leading you to your life's work.

One woman always loved beautiful towels, linens, and unusual bathroom and bedroom knick-knacks. She shopped all over for unusual articles, even sending for items from overseas. One day it occurred to her that she could open her own shop, for she knew from experience that no existing shop sold as many beautiful and unusual things as she had found. She opened a small, successful retail store and later put together a mail-order business for others like herself who wanted hard-to-find and unusual items. You can turn the activities you love to do into a successful business; there are many people who have done so.

I *honor and value my creativity and ideas.*

If you have ideas about what you might do with your life, yet feel they are not good enough, find something in your life that you value and begin to value it even more. If you value your ability to help people or to organize things, focus on that skill. Learn to value yourself and your talents. Treat yourself as if you count, for you do. Start in small ways to value your path and the things you love to do. You can do simple things, such as allowing yourself ten minutes to sit quietly and think without interruptions. You can choose to spend less time talking to people or doing things you don't enjoy and use the time to do something special for yourself. You can allow yourself to spend more time on a hobby you love, or buy yourself the equipment you need to do it well. As you do these things you give a message to yourself that your life and work are important.

Learn to value your special skills. One man found it easy to work for others, but found it hard to spend time doing things for himself. Although he had many good ideas about what he wanted to do, he was plagued by doubts, thinking that what he loved to do wasn't worth devoting time to. It was easy for him to spend all of his weekends and evenings helping other people but difficult to put any time into carrying out his dreams.

He decided to start valuing his ideas. He started in small ways, asserting himself more and taking more time for himself. He had always loved to teach, and he was very drawn to nature, constantly taking walks and reading books about flowers and trees. He enjoyed identifying plants as he walked, and loved being outdoors. He went to the parks and recreation department in his city and found that they offered guided tours through the national parks nearby. He started by volunteering his time on weekends, and soon found himself spending all his spare time leading both adult and children's groups, teaching them about nature. Soon he was getting paid to lead backpacking trips through wilderness areas and was in much demand as a weekend guide.

He began to realize he could accept money for doing what he loved. He started to honor his time. As he began to value his knowledge of nature and his love of the outdoors, so did those around him. He found many opportunities to make money and support himself while doing what he loved.

He was offered a full-time job creating and running outdoor programs at a children's camp and eventually became its owner.

One woman had extensively studied and worked with the use of colors for promoting emotional well-being. She had redecorated her home in harmonious, soothing colors, and had built a wardrobe around the colors that brought her emotional well-being. She found her friends constantly asking for advice on the use of colors for their homes and clothes. She began to realize that their questions were taking up a lot of her time. She started in small ways to honor herself, and began to see that her time was valuable and her knowledge useful.

Although she was timid about it at first, she got the courage to suggest that friends who asked for advice set up appointments with her. For a small hourly fee she would sit down and work with them, going over what they wanted to accomplish and helping them find ways to do so. At first her friends were surprised by the change, but they soon realized that she gave them more attention and was therefore more helpful when they paid. Because she began to honor her talent, she was able to eventually make it a full-time career, acquiring more skills, knowledge, and training along the way. Businesses began to ask her advice on office and hotel color schemes, and she became a professional color consultant.

I *am a special, unique person.*

Some of you aren't doing your life's work out of fear that you or your skills are inadequate, or that in some way other people have something special to offer that you don't. You have been given the talents, desires, skills, and preferences you have because they are in some way a part of your path and needed in the world. Much important work is waiting for you to wake up to your purpose and believe in yourself. Your work is important; your contribution is special and needed.

When your doubts come up, if the voices within you tell you that your skills and talents are not worth investing time and energy in, send love to those thoughts. Don't fight them mentally, don't try to reason with them or argue them away. Tell yourself it is all right to have those thoughts. Let them be there, and place a confident, positive thought alongside your thoughts of doubt.

Spend your leisure time reading books or taking courses that will prepare you for greater success. You may want to spend time with other people who are doing what you would like to do, an excellent way to accelerate your success in any field. This might mean enrolling in their classes, or seeking them out as teachers, counselors, or advisors. You might want to read about others who have succeeded in doing what you want to do. Surround yourself with inspiration and constantly renew your enthusiasm.

For instance, one man wanted to be a real estate developer, though he had a job in another field. He began to go to community meetings attended by developers, as well as to their association meetings. He listened to them, began to make friends, and started acquiring many skills and ideas as a result of being in that environment. Eventually at one of the meetings he heard about a small piece of real estate that was a perfect project for him to begin a career with.

When you put yourself around people who are successfully doing what you want to do, you pick up their verbal and telepathic thoughts of success. As you do, you accelerate the development of your image of yourself as a success. Since your thoughts create your reality, the more you picture yourself successfully doing what you love, the more rapidly it will come about.

M*y days are filled with fun and meaningful activities.*

Many of you hold yourselves back from your life's work, thinking that it's going to be hard to do. You think, perhaps, of how much work it took to do other jobs that weren't your life's work. You cannot compare the two. It takes much more energy to do even simple work that you are not suited to than to do vast, complex work that your life's path may involve. As you do your life's work, the universe will be helping you. Doors will open and opportunities will come your way. You will be flowing with the current rather than against it.

In some ways pursuing your life's work is like developing an intimate relationship; success requires a bonding and commitment to it, and an ability to surrender to wherever it takes you. Some of you think that once you are committed to your path your life will no longer be fun, that you will have to be responsible and serious all the time. You do not have to be serious and stop having fun to do your life's work. In fact, you will discover that when you are not doing your life's work life is not as much fun. Once you are doing your life's work your days will be filled with fun and meaningful, joyful activities.

PLAYSHEET

1 | What inner resource or strength could you develop that would help draw your life's work to you more rapidly? Or, if you are already doing your life's work, what inner resource or strength could you develop that would help you move to your next level?

2 | What one step could you take in the next week to express that inner resource or strength more fully?

3 | Think of as many activities as you can that you do right now that you enjoy. You may want to refer to your answers to the first question in the playsheet, *Discovering Your Life's Work* from the preceding chapter.

4 | Pick one of the above activities. List five ways you might create money from this activity you love. Don't censor these ideas; be creative.

CHAPTER 15

*B*elieving *in Y*ourself

To create your life's work, believe in yourself and act upon your ideas. If you are waiting for friends, your husband or wife, employer, employees, or co-workers to give you what you want, you are turning your power over to others. For instance, if you are waiting for your employer to change your job to your liking or give you the raise you want, you are setting yourself up for possible disappointment. Take the initiative to change your job yourself, within the guidelines set by your company. Increase your productivity and improve your performance. Decide that if, despite your efforts, you can't get your needs met where you are, you will find another job that does meet your needs. Examine other jobs and alternatives that might offer you what you want.

I give myself permission to be all I can be.

Are you waiting for someone to give you money or to decide that you can go to school, get a job, or make a change that you want to make? Give yourself permission to do what you want to do with your life. Decide you are going to take action toward your goal. Don't wait for someone else to give you permission to quit your job and do what you love with your life. If you give up your goals, dreams, and aliveness to be with people, you aren't truly doing them a favor. You will in some way demand that they give up the same thing. The only way you can truly love and support others is to support their aliveness and growth, and one of the best ways to do that is to support your own aliveness and growth. Give yourself permission to do what you love and want to do.

True love is serving people's souls, not their personalities. For instance, one man did not want his wife to get a job, although she felt it would bring her much joy and aliveness. He thought he made enough money to support the family and wanted her to stay home and take care of the house and the family's needs. She was pulled between staying home and going back to work, because she had always felt compelled to take care of others. She began to look at the situation through the eyes of her soul, and she saw that she was not serving her husband's soul; she was serving only his personality, his smaller self and not his greater self.

She knew that by going to work, by growing, becoming happy, and increasing her aliveness, she would be much more powerful and that her power would empower him as well, even if he didn't believe so at the time. She knew that at the soul level the greatest gift she could give him was to be all that she could be, for it would free him to be all that he could be as well. She realized that any time you hold another person back, you are also holding yourself back, and by trying to hold her back her husband was at some level holding himself back. So she got a job.

He was not happy with her decision, objected loudly, and gave her many reasons why it would not work. He made it difficult for her to go to work, complaining frequently and not helping her in any way. She kept reminding herself that she was serving his soul, and if one of them broke through to a new level of personal power and higher purpose it would help the other one do so also. She still had moments of feeling that she was being selfish by going to work, but the inner joy of learning made her feel so alive that she knew she couldn't sacrifice that aliveness and still love herself or him.

Eventually they were able to use some of her income to pay off their debts, and even take a long-postponed and much needed vacation. He stopped complaining about her working, and even began to like the changes in their lives. He was able to spend some money on a hobby he had wanted to pursue, and his sense of aliveness began increasing. A few years later he decided to quit his job, which he had not liked for a long time, and go into business for himself. Although it was a risk and meant less income in the beginning, they were able to take the risk because her salary, combined with a loan, was enough to launch his new career. Her willingness to pursue her path eventually made it possible for her husband to pursue his life's work. Her commitment to her aliveness brought them both more aliveness.

I *commit to my path.*
I choose aliveness and growth.

You may encounter resistance from people around you as you begin to move in the direction of your aliveness and growth. It is often threatening to people close to you when you choose to grow or change. They fear a loss of your love. Rather than feeling threatened by their resistance, send them extra love and compassion.

Sometimes having someone oppose you can actually be a gift. In overcoming the resistance of others, you often strengthen your resolve and develop more courage and greater commitment to your path. You may have noticed that when someone tells you you can't do something, you sometimes make up your mind to prove you can.

If you have well-meaning friends who tell you that something is hard to do or can't be done, realize that they are only showing you your own doubts, mirroring them back to you so you may become more aware of them and let them go. As you deal with their objections, you are really dealing with your own doubts and fears. When you feel clear about your path, others will usually mirror your confidence back to you. Rather than getting angry with them for not believing in you, thank them mentally for showing you your doubts and helping you strengthen your resolve and will.

One couple was preparing to open a restaurant, and had practiced all of the principles of manifesting. They had energized the symbol of their life's work, followed their inner messages, taken step after step, and were certain their direction was to open a restaurant. They magnetized clients, visualized the perfect location, and did the appropriate exercises to release any inner blocks to their abundance and prosperity.

All their friends told them it would be difficult, if not impossible, to succeed. They were told that restaurants seldom make money and have a high failure rate, and that running one would involve long, hard hours. They realized that their friends were mirroring back to them their own doubts, and so they used their friends' comments as feedback about what fears and doubts they needed to release. They kept checking their inner messages, which continued to point to a restaurant as their path.

They decided to open a small restaurant, and found a good location. In the middle of their negotiations to buy the building, the deal fell through, even after they visualized taking ownership and affirmed that it would be theirs. They wondered if their friends were right, and whether the universe was trying to stop them. Their inner messages kept pointing to continuing, so they looked for and found another location. It turned out to be a perfect place, and they realized that they had been protected from buying the other place, which wasn't nearly as appropriate.

One positive event after another occurred. They got much unexpected and helpful publicity, for theirs was the first restaurant of its kind in the area. The restaurant did so well within the first three months that they were able to hire more help and work less themselves. They made more money than they ever expected to make, and gained much valuable business experience. She was able to take time off to have a baby and stay home with her child, something she had always dreamed about.

I *follow my heart.*

Don't let other people's pictures of what you ought to be doing determine what you do. You may want to pursue a career in music while your parents want you to become a business executive. Realize they mean well and want to see you succeed, but only you can know what your path is. Your life's work may be quite different from what others picture you doing. It is important to honor your own direction. To succeed at anything you must love it, and only you can know what you love. If you go against your inner messages, trying to succeed at a career you don't love just to please others, you will lose your sense of joy and aliveness. Decide that you will do whatever you are receiving the impulse to do with your life, even if you don't see how there can be any money in it. If it feels right, honors your integrity, and brings you joy, do it. Success comes when you follow your heart.

It is best to follow your own wisdom. If things turn out well, you will know that you did it yourself, and have even more trust and confidence in yourself in the future. If things don't turn out as you expect, you will have gained much knowledge and experience that will help you make better choices in the future. Either way, you gain much more by following your own wisdom than by doing what others think you ought to do.

I *can have what I want.*

There are no excuses for not acting upon your dreams. Some of you blame others for your inability to act on your dreams, saying "I am not free; my husband or my wife won't let me; I have too many responsibilities to my children or parents." If you keep telling yourself why you can't have what you want, you won't have it. Begin to tell yourself why you CAN have what you want. There are always actions you can take right now to make your dreams become a reality. You always have a choice, for no matter how boxed in or trapped you feel by any situation, there is always a way out.

Take a moment to think about what you would love to do with your life. Are you waiting for anyone to give you permission to do it, or to help you out before you begin? If so, are you willing to give yourself permission to do what you want? Do so now. Are you holding back because someone in your life doesn't support what you want to do? The process of discovering your life's work and learning to believe in yourself enough to act upon your inner messages is just as important as doing the work. If someone came along and handed everything to you, you wouldn't have the strength that comes from doing it yourself. You are the captain of the ship; your success comes from you.

I *invite and allow good to come into my life.*

In order to improve your life, first believe that something better exists. Many people think that what they have now is the best they can create and fear making any changes. Start by at least believing that circumstances could be better, that you can have what you want, that it is all right to do what you love with your life. There is always a way that your circumstances can be changed. Take a moment to think of at least three reasons why you CAN have what you want.

You may need to create time to develop and use your higher skills. This means spending your day doing those tasks that only you can do, and letting others help with the rest. One woman started a small business offering typing services to other small businesses, but she didn't have the time to expand her business or to service clients as well as she wanted. She was too busy and tired from trying to run the business as well as doing the typing, housework, errands, cooking, and many other tasks. One day she realized that she needed to find help, but worried that she wouldn't be able to pay someone and still show a profit. She then decided that during the time she was paying someone to do housework, she would use her higher skills and generate at least twice as much money as she paid for the help.

Taking a leap of faith, she hired someone to help her. She spent her free time organizing the business, getting clients, and looking after their needs. Before she had been too tired to truly serve people or to acquire new business, but now she had the time. People noticed her attention to their needs and excellent service, and she got many referrals and repeat customers. Not only was she better able to serve more people and make more money, she was also able to provide a job doing typing and housework for someone who needed and appreciated the work.

Some people worry that they are too old to change careers or to activate their life's work. You are never too old. Many people have founded major businesses after the age of sixty. One woman who had been in her job for many years wanted to find more meaningful work. She was close to retirement and had been with the company for many years. She felt that she could endure the last few years, even though she had long since ceased to grow and feel challenged in this job, but she longed for a more satisfying job.

She began to focus every day on creating her higher purpose, energizing her symbol, which was a circle of light. She began to think positively, believing that it might be possible to find a better job, even though she didn't see how at the time. In the meantime, she began dating a wonderful man, and together they explored many things. He had a company that he had started several years after retirement for fun, and hadn't expected it to grow as rapidly as it had. Her skills were perfect for his business. He not only hired her to work for him full time, but they also ended up getting married. It was everything she had asked for and more; she loved the work, was part of a team, felt challenged, and was learning new skills.

PLAYSHEET

1 | Imagine that it is ten years from today. You have given yourself permission to be all you can be; you have believed in yourself; you have taken the appropriate steps to follow your higher path. How do you feel about yourself and your life? Make up a fantasy about the success of your last ten years.

2 | Now imagine the same ten-year period. You did not give yourself permission to follow your own path; you did not believe in yourself. How do you feel about your life?

3 | Which path will you choose? Decide now.

CHAPTER 16

*T*rusting the *F*low

Is a job, career, or situation that used to work no longer working for you? Perhaps what you once loved to do has become a "have to" or lost its sense of newness and aliveness. Perhaps you have experienced a drop in sales or clients, or a lack of enthusiasm for something you used to enjoy. No matter what level of prosperity and abundance you have achieved, there may come a time when your picture of where you want to be, or think you ought to be, does not match where you are. This can happen to anyone, those who have millions of dollars and those who wonder where their next meal will come from.

It is important to know when it is time to change course. No job, business, or activity will be perfect forever unless you are willing to constantly update it, for as you grow the things around you need to be revised. Sometimes a simple change will do. Other times the only way you will be able to go to the next level will be to let go of everything you have and start over with something completely different.

I flow with the current.
I know that everything happens
for my higher good.

There are natural phases to the creation of all things. The first phase is the idea stage. You are brimming with ideas, new thinking, and a desire for change, even though you may not see how you can create it. The next phase is the building phase, when you see ways to put your ideas into action and do so. Manifesting what you have been desiring is exciting. This phase is followed by the completion of what you are building, a leveling-off phase during which your ideas are working but are no longer expanding and growing. The next phase is the ending of one cycle and the beginning of the next. You may feel dissatisfied with what you have built; perhaps it is no longer the vehicle that can take you to your new, expanded goals.

Many of you think of this last phase as a downward cycle. In truth it is part of a natural cycle of birth, death, and rebirth. It is the old leaving, paving the way for the new. If things aren't working as well as you would like right now, if you aren't as happy as you used to be with your career, you may be getting ready to expand and move up to a new level.

The job you have now and the skills you use were appropriate to bring you your original goals. If you are now asking for more, thinking in bigger and more expansive ways, you may need a new vehicle to get you where you want to go next. The same job, thoughts, skills, or attitudes will bring you only what you now have. You need to discover new ways of thinking or feeling, new perspectives, skills, and ideas, for you are getting ready to start a new cycle. You have not failed or gone backward. Instead, see yourself as a success; you are getting ready for a new leap forward.

No path is ever closed or slowed down unless that is for your higher good. If following your path is a struggle, if it is getting too difficult, take time to reexamine what you are doing. There may be a better way to do things, or something else entirely different may be emerging for you. If one path is giving you difficulty, there is another path you can follow, and it will hold even more aliveness and abundance than the one you are on.

I *am alert to my opportunities and I use them well.*

Remember that the current of mankind's evolution is a constantly changing course and that circumstances are always changing. What mankind wants now and what people are excited about now is not the same as it was even a year ago. Even the best of plans must be constantly revised. You will need to check in and see if your pictures are still in alignment with your inner directions and the direction in which mankind is going. An airplane that is flying to its destination must constantly readjust its flight path to stay on course. You may find that you need to constantly update what you are doing to stay closely aligned with the course of man.

Once you create something, you will need to learn how to let it grow and evolve. What works for you today may not work for you at a future time without some revision. What you feel guided to do now may not be what you are guided to do during the following months or years. You will need to take risks, try new activities, and stay in touch with your energy. When you are no longer enjoying what you are doing, it is a sign that something new is needed. If this is so, developing the new will bring you more abundance than holding on to the old. You are always changing and growing, and as you stay in touch with what you enjoy doing you will draw to you the new forms that match who you are.

Creating your life's work doesn't come from choosing safety and comfort over growth. It comes from choosing and taking those actions that help you get to where you want to go. Learn to embrace your challenges with love rather than avoiding them. Start by doing something that is a slight reach for you; take on a slightly more challenging project than you normally tackle, or learn a new skill. When you do things that make you reach, the rewards are great. You will feel invigorated and energized afterward. Take the level of risk that is comfortable for you, and increase it by one level. You do not need to take steps that are extremely uncomfortable, for that is not the path of joy, but do increase your willingness to risk as a way of attracting more to you.

I *release anything that is not for my higher good and ask it to release me.*

The way you deal with the old patterns leaving determines how much pain or struggle you will experience during this phase. Sometimes you may merely need to let go of an attitude or belief. Sometimes you may need to release the job you have and find a new one. You can leave what you have created joyfully, willingly, and consciously, or you can wait until circumstances reach crisis proportions and you are "forced" to implement new ideas. If it is time to make changes but you are reluctant to let go of the old, your soul will help you by creating circumstances in which the old no longer works.

You have changed and grown in the process of getting what you wanted. Your goals may be bigger or different now and the things you created may no longer challenge you the way they did before. Life always seeks a higher order, and once you have achieved one goal, you will usually be looking toward the next goal. Some of you let go easily and naturally, implementing your new ideas and letting go of old forms when it is appropriate. Some of you keep trying to make the old forms work, putting more and more effort into them, until you decide to look at new forms and ideas, starting the cycle all over again. It is the nature of all life to go toward growth and aliveness. Once you have mastered one level, you are ready to go on to the next.

You can decide how much discontent and dissatisfaction motivates you to act on your inner messages. Some of you continuously create the jobs and lives you want, constantly striving to give yourselves environments that support your aliveness. You change your circumstances when you hear the whispers, letting go of the old easily and embracing new directions as they emerge.

Some of you do not make changes until you experience discontent or anxiety. If you are in the latter category, your soul may create more and more problems, discomfort, or internal resistance toward your existing job or situation to get you to pay attention to the fact that changes need to be made. Learn to let go of the old or find ways to change things when you stop loving what you are doing, and when you are no longer growing and feeling alive from doing it.

It is a challenge to love rather than dislike what you are leaving. If you focus on what you want, what you would love to have, and go toward it, you will have it. The more you dislike something, the more you may be stuck with it. The more you dislike your business, the longer you may be in it. One of the principles of your universe is that every situation in your life is teaching you how to love. You cannot leave something until you love it. You are tied to things you don't like. If you hate something, you will be drawn to it again and again (even though the person or form may change) until you love it. Once you love it, you are free from it.

I *love and honor everything I create.*

A man started a business of his own, and discovered a year later that he didn't like it. He hadn't anticipated the long hours, the lack of money, or the kinds of people he would have to deal with. He wished he was in another business. He began avoiding the office, did not return calls, and because the business wasn't doing well, he went further and further into debt. As his debts increased, he had fewer options about what he could do with his company or his life.

One day a friend told him, "You can't be free of something until you love it," and in desperation he decided to try loving his business. He returned calls, spent extra time with clients, and spent days getting the company into excellent condition, organizing all the records, implementing cost-effective and time-saving procedures, and much more. Within two months the company began making a profit, and within a year he had enough money to start another business in a different field, one much more to his liking. Because he loved his first business, it did well and developed a good reputation, and he was able to sell it for a nice profit.

I *let go easily,*
trusting that nothing leaves my life
unless something better is coming.

PLAYSHEET

1 | Think of some aspect of your life, job, or career that once worked well and is not working as well as it was or is leaving. This might be a drop in business or sales, a task that has become burdensome, or a project that is ending. If there is no place in your life where you are letting go, leaving, or finishing something, go to the next chapter.

2 | What was your self-image when you started this aspect of your life? How has your self-image changed since then? Have your goals become larger or changed in some way? What new vision do you have of yourself and your direction in this area?

3 | What changes has your inner self been urging you to make? These changes might come to you in the form of ideas, dreams, thoughts, or pictures of activities you would like to do.

4 | Given your new vision and any urgings of your inner self, what new directions might be emerging? Do you think these new directions can be made within the structure you now have, or might you need a new structure?

5 | Pick a new direction that may be emerging and imagine that it is one year from today. You have developed this idea, built upon it, incorporated it into your life, and released any conflicting directions. From this future vantage point, describe how well your life is going and how glad you are you paid attention and acted upon the new direction that was emerging.

CHAPTER 17

*M*oving to
*Y*our *H*igher *P*ath

You may have come to the point at which you need to make certain choices and decisions. If it is time to change the old and build the new, you will want to examine what is the best step to take. Is it time to leave or transform your existing job? Start your own business? Get a job? Go to school to acquire additional knowledge and skills?

You do not necessarily need to quit the job you have to get your new work or ideas out to the world. Stay where you are while you begin to take action on your new ideas. Let them have time to germinate and grow at their own speed. Remain in your present job until you have built a foundation for your new work that is solid enough to support you. If you were building a new house, you would want to stay in your old house until the new one was complete enough to move into.

It is often better not to link issues of your survival with the new direction you are taking. Don't let your need for monthly income put pressure on you as you begin your new path. Instead, find a way to bring in sufficient income while you do all the things you can think of to put your ideas into action and to make your new path as strong as possible.

If your current job doesn't satisfy you, you may want to transform it rather than leave it. Many of you have good jobs that could be more satisfying if you were willing to change your attitude or work on making the job more suitable to you. It is rare to step into a job and find that everything is perfect; part of your challenge is to make the job fit who you are. If you are complaining about your work, what exactly are you unhappy with? Some people leave good jobs simply because they don't like something about their employer, a co-worker, or some small thing about the job. If you feel your current job is making a contribution, is meaningful, and offers you opportunities to grow, it may be worth working on making the job better. If you do not enjoy what you are doing now, that doesn't mean it can't become enjoyable.

I *change the world around me by changing myself.*

You can change many situations you do not like by changing something within yourself. The ways people treat you and the opportunities that come your way are determined by your attitudes, energy, and love. If you are not feeling nurtured at your job, it may be because you are not nurturing yourself. If you feel unappreciated by your employer, co-workers, or employees, it may be that you have not learned to appreciate yourself. Once you learn to nurture and appreciate yourself, you will find others do so also. Before you quit your job, look at what you don't like about it and ask if what you are experiencing might be a reflection of how you treat yourself. If you don't change the behavior that created this situation, you may create similar situations in any job you hold.

If you want to receive something, start by giving something first. If you want respect, start giving respect to yourself and others. If you want to improve your job, don't ask what your employer can do for you; ask instead, "What can I contribute to my job?" What you get out of your job might change dramatically if you contribute your highest and best, work with a good attitude, do more than you are asked to do, and anticipate what needs to be done without being asked.

Those who serve others and make a great deal of money at the same time are people who go to work with an attitude of joy, love what they do, are willing to put in extra hours, and care about the well-being of those they serve. Develop the trait of putting forth your best wherever you are and it will bring you greater abundance.

A woman who worked for a large company initially enjoyed her job but had recently begun to feel overwhelmed by the workload and started disliking it. She was thinking of quitting and confided her unhappiness in her job to her boss. Being wise, he asked her to make a list of all the tasks her job entailed and to look at what she liked and disliked about it. As she began evaluating what she spent her time doing, she realized that she spent most of her time doing small tasks rather than the larger, more meaningful tasks she enjoyed. She hadn't wanted to inconvenience others, so she had not delegated work or asked for help. She saw that although she had been blaming others for giving her too much to do, she needed to learn to nurture herself before she could receive nurturing from others. She decided to make some changes.

She looked at which tasks associated with her job she loved and which she didn't love. She realized that the things she didn't like weren't really using her higher skills, and that they could be delegated to someone else who would be challenged by and enjoy those tasks. As she let go of trying to do everything and focused instead on using her higher skills, she became a greater asset to the company, coming up with many creative and innovative ideas. She also began to love her job. As she nurtured herself, she found herself being nurtured by the job. By making changes in herself, she transformed the job into one that brought her joy.

If you dislike going to work every day, if you don't agree with your company's goals and philosophy, aren't sincerely committed to doing your best, don't enjoy what you do or your co-workers, your job is not truly making a contribution to your life. It is time to look for another job. Be honest with yourself. Do you basically like your job but dislike certain elements of it? If you go to work every day thinking how much you dislike your job, if the problems in your office are beyond your ability to solve, you are not listening to your inner guidance that something better awaits you. Many people stay in jobs long after their positions stop providing them with growth and aliveness, thinking that there is nothing better for them.

I *bring love and a positive attitude to everything I do.*

Whether or not you are working in your perfect job, learn to view what you do with love and a positive attitude. As you do, you will find yourself either creating a better situation within your current company or finding opportunities elsewhere. Every uncomfortable situation is teaching you valuable lessons you need to learn. If you do not learn the lessons in the job you have, you will create similar situations in your new job to teach you the same lessons.

Identify what you don't like in your current job and begin to work on it now, knowing as you master an uncomfortable situation in this job you will not need to create it again. Look at your job and make a list of all of the gifts it is giving you, all the lessons it is teaching you, and all the skills you use in doing it. When you appreciate and love where you are, it is easier to create your next step.

After examining your current job, you may decide it is time for a change. You may want to work for another company in a similar field that allows you more opportunities to grow. You may want to change to a different field altogether. If you aren't currently employed, you may decide that you want to get a job. If you have been developing a hobby or another interest, it may be time to turn that into a career.

You do not have to work hard to get the job you want, but you need to be clear about what you want. As you energize the symbol of your life's work and get clear about the essence of your perfect job, your higher self will go out to the world and put all the pieces together, bringing you coincidences, people, opportunities, and usually the job itself.

I *create what I want easily and effortlessly.*

If you are looking for a job, remember that there is an abundance of good jobs available. It is not true that there aren't enough good jobs. What is true is that most people don't know how to find them. Some of the most important steps you can take, after getting clear about what you want, are to do energy work and start magnetizing the job you want as you picture yourself having it.

You don't need to know what the job title will be to find your ideal work. You can begin by observing what you do naturally and easily and draw to you those jobs that will allow you to do the activities you love. Once you have a clear model of what your job will give you, you can begin to work with energy to draw it to you. Your higher self will work on finding it, bringing to you whatever job title is most appropriate. It may be a job you haven't even thought of, or didn't know existed.

To find this job, pay attention to your intuition; get quiet and listen to your inner messages. Some people get into a flurry of activity and don't take time to listen to their inner messages. You could go out and look for your new job in the want ads, and you could work hard to find it. Or, since you have worked with energy first, you can follow your intuition and find your ideal job in the easiest way possible, taking only the action you have the guidance to take. After you do energy work to draw your job to you, your intuition may still tell you to go to employment agencies or look at want ads. If it does, your efforts will be fruitful and lead you to your job rather than to frustration.

A woman was looking for a job and was very clear about what she wanted—the hours, type of work, environment, and people she wanted to work with. She kept feeling guilty for not working harder to get a new job, but it seemed like an inner voice told her not to go out and work on it. She stayed at the job she had for a bit longer and began to change her attitude. She decided that if she was going to continue working at the same place, she was going to be cheerful and love what she was doing, even though she had found the work tedious and boring before.

As she began to focus on joy, she became more magnetic to people. Good things began to happen in other areas of her life. Although she put her heart into the job she had, she always kept sight of the new job she wanted. One day an old friend she hadn't seen in a long time asked her out to lunch. Her inner voice said to go, even though she had many chores to do that afternoon. It turned out that her friend was in business for himself and had recently done work for a client who was looking for someone to fill a position. The job was exactly what she had been looking for. She met his client, and was hired for the job.

You may decide that you want to start your own business rather than work for someone else. The jobs you want may not exist until you create them. Those of you who do best in your own businesses like responsibility and making decisions, want a lot of independence and freedom, like challenge and risk-taking, and enjoy working alone. You are resourceful, self-reliant, flexible, like to be assertive, are thorough, and able to do a wide variety of jobs. You like to use many different skills in such areas as management, sales, accounting, hiring and training people, organizing, and putting in and maintaining new systems. You like to set your own vision and direction, and enjoy some degree of uncertainty.

I *am magnetic to my higher good and it is magnetic to me.*

If you are thinking of going into business for yourself, we have included energy exercises in this book in Section 1, *Creating Money*, to magnetize clients to you and to help you attract increasing opportunities to serve greater and greater numbers of people. We encourage you to be knowledgeable about the man-made laws of creating money as well. There are many good books available on running a business; read those that find their way to you.

Starting your own business will require your alertness, attention, and awareness. New ideas will be coming in rapidly, and many will require you to try new things and think in new ways. Even though you may think you can't wait to achieve your goals, remember that getting there is half the fun. Enjoy this building phase, for it is an exciting adventure, leading you down new paths full of growth and aliveness. If you are interested in going into business for yourself, think about all the reasons why you will succeed. Start with your personality, skills, and motivation. Believe in yourself, for you can have what you want.

As you start doing the things you love, you may discover that you need additional skills and knowledge to do the job you have decided on. You may feel drawn to going to school or furthering your education in some way as the next step in your life's work. Don't assume that you need certification or a degree in order to get a particular job. You may want to explore getting a job in the field of your choice before you automatically assume you need to go to school. You may find work that will give you on-the-job training. Ask yourself if the process of studying and learning sounds joyful. Or is it the job you want to have after finishing school that sounds joyful, and the schooling just something to endure in order to get the job you want?

If it sounds joyful to go to school, if you love the idea, then it is appropriate to do so. If you really have no interest in going to school but it looks like the only way to get a job that pays well, your life's work will not require you to go to school. Your lack of enthusiasm is your soul's way of directing you to another path. You can begin to do what you want without the credentials you think you need.

Remember that employers want someone who is conscientious, loyal, enthusiastic, and dedicated as much as you want a job. Good employees are like gold, highly valued and treasured. Your attitude is one of the most important qualities you bring to your job, in many cases more important than your credentials or experience. Most companies would rather hire a less experienced person who learns quickly and is brimming with enthusiasm than a highly trained individual who is unenthusiastic.

If you don't want to go to school, get in touch with the essence of what you think it will give you, and begin drawing that to you. For instance, one woman wanted to become a doctor, but it didn't feel joyful to her to spend years getting the education that was required. She began to examine the essence of what she wanted, which was to heal people. She made a symbol for this and began to energize it. She then followed her inner messages and found herself being drawn toward body work. She began taking classes, and enjoyed them so much she took all of them she could find in various fields. She studied with some of the best teachers, and after several years began a successful and growing practice. She worked with people, helping them to heal themselves, and found great joy in her work.

If you do decide that going back to school is your path, you may wonder how to find the money or time to do so. There is plenty of money available to help you further your education, but most people do not know it is available or are not willing to take the time to find out where it is. Take the time to magnetize the money, and then take action based on your inner messages. Remember, if you are getting the inner message to go back to school, there will always be ways to do so.

A man who had dropped out of high school and then worked as a warehouseman for several years decided that he wanted to go back to school and get a college education in engineering. He didn't know how he was going to pay for it, or even get accepted without a high school diploma, but he started by believing that it would be possible to do so. He visualized himself going back to school, and made a symbol and energized it. He picked a college, and decided to enroll for the fall semester, six months away.

He sent for a catalog of class schedules, and began planning his courses. He decided to take advantage of the school's career counseling services, and made friends with a counselor. The counselor helped him research scholarships, and he discovered that the school had a program that gave financial assistance to people who had not completed high school. To be eligible for this particular scholarship one must have worked for several years, which he had. The program even included the courses he would need to complete his high school diploma. He was able to quit his job and go back to school full time in the fall, just as he had pictured. He did get his degree in engineering, and was able to get a very good job when he graduated.

I *am abundantly provided for*
as I follow my path.

Never let the thought that you need a lot of money to launch your business, go back to school, or embark upon your career stop you. Begin to do the things you can do right now as if you will have all the money you need. One woman wanted to be a singer. She thought that to be a singer she needed thousands of dollars worth of expensive equipment and a huge savings account to live off of while she made a name for herself. For a long time she kept working at jobs she didn't like, hoping to save enough money to eventually start a singing career.

One day she realized that she was getting further and further away from her dream, and she would never be a singer if she didn't start. She began to take singing lessons at night and to associate with people who were already successfully doing what she wanted to do. After a year, one of the bands she was friendly with lost one of its singers and invited her to take the woman's place. She didn't need any money for equipment, and she made enough income to quit her job and sing as a full-time career.

If you have done everything possible to energize your work, know that it is coming. Continue to energize your symbol and ask your wiser, deeper self to send you new ideas. Be willing to listen to and act upon the insights and new ideas you receive. Don't wait for the money. It is not a lack of money that stops you. It may be that you don't believe in yourself or your idea enough to have yet attracted the money, or you may not believe that you deserve to have what you want. Write down your ideas. As you put your plans on paper, as you design and build them, you will draw to you the people and financial assistance that can help you. There is more money available than there are good projects to invest in. You will create all the necessary contacts, steps, and events with your intention and vision. You will find that anything you need to serve your life's work will come to you. When you are on your path doing your life's work, all you need is abundantly supplied.

MOVING TO YOUR HIGHER PATH
PLAYSHEET

1 | If you have a decision to make about your career right now (such as whether to go back to school, find a job, or change jobs or careers) state it below.

2 | List all your possible options and choices. Think big; think of your fantasy life.

3 | Get quiet and go within. Which option feels the most alive and joyful as you think about doing it? Don't worry how you will do it.

4 | Take the option that has the most aliveness and joy for you and list in one column all the reasons you can do it and in another column all the reasons you can't do it.

5 | Now, take all the reasons you think you can't follow this choice, and make them positive affirmations. For instance, "I can't go back to school because I don't have the money" can be changed to "I can go back to school and I now have the money." "I can't get a job because I don't have any marketable skills" can be changed to "I can get a job because my past experiences, skills, and abilities are useful and valuable." You are creating your own positive affirmations as you do this.

Having Money

Honoring Your Value and Worth

Joy and Appreciation

Giving and Receiving

Clarity and Harmony

Having Money

Savings: Affirming Your Abundance

CHAPTER 18

Honoring Your Value and Worth

It is important to receive what you think your services are worth, in money or whatever medium is of value to you. If you do not value your time and energy, you cut off your flow of abundance. Your energy determines whether or not money flows freely, harmoniously, and easily for you. There are many ways you can open the flow. You automatically create a smooth flow of money and abundance when you do things that honor you and others, and when you receive what you feel you are worth in return for your time and services.

Many people are disappointed with the pay or exchange they receive for their services because they are not clear themselves on what their services are worth. They hope that other people will see their value and give them more. Many people hope they will get a raise or expect their clients to offer them more than they ask for, even though they never speak about their feelings. When you value your services, others will value them also. Determine for yourself what your time is worth, what income or exchange is meaningful to you. Do not depend upon others to do this for you. It is important that both you and the person paying you feel the arrangement is fair; everyone wants to feel he or she is getting a fair exchange.

Many of you say, "I will reduce my fee to get more clients or sales." Make sure you do not constantly cut your fee below what you feel your services are worth. If you cut your fee and do not feel good about it, you are cutting off the flow of money in two ways. First, there may be an undercurrent of resentment or bad feeling which, even if it is small, will stop money from coming back to you. Second, you are telling your subconscious that your work is not worth that much, and it will stop bringing you opportunities. Learn to be more loving to yourself by receiving your worth.

I *know my value. I honor my worth.*

If you are in business for yourself, it is better for you to have two clients who pay you what you feel your services are worth than four who do not. When you receive fair value for what you do, you feel good about yourself; you radiate enthusiasm. A business person who radiates enthusiasm, prosperity, and success is more effective in serving people than one who is feeling poor, depleted, and unsuccessful.

Decide that you will receive what you are worth. Don't worry that you might go bankrupt from raising your prices or not be able to create enough customers who value your work. People who raise their prices to reflect their worth seldom lose many customers. They often find that in their sense of renewed enthusiasm and excitement they offer even more to people than before. Whether or not you raise your prices, make sure you give as much service as possible to those you serve; give them good value for their money.

If you are receiving a salary or commission, are you receiving what you think you are worth? What income would you like to be making? What benefits would you like to be receiving? To earn this increased amount, you may need to give more to your company, increase your skills in some way, or offer extra services. You may want to become even more self-motivated, taking on work without being asked, anticipating and meeting needs before they are voiced, and giving your best. If you are doing these things and you still aren't receiving what you feel you deserve, make up your mind that you will, and write a date on your calendar when you want to receive your increased amount. Don't wait for anyone to give it to you; that is turning over your fate to someone else. Be willing to change jobs if you cannot receive what you want at your current job. Making what you feel you are worth will increase your sense of aliveness and joy, and will be a gift to those around you.

One of the greatest rewards is knowing you are making a meaningful contribution to society, that you are helping people to create better lives for themselves. Many people take jobs that pay less but offer them the opportunity to help make the world a better place. If you are involved in community service, or making less in one field than you could in another, you may be receiving nonfinancial rewards that are even greater than the financial ones you could receive elsewhere.

The energy that comes back to you when you make a meaningful contribution to the world around you is a reward even greater than money, for it allows you to grow spiritually, open your heart, gain compassion, and live a valuable and rewarding life. In this case, honoring your worth would mean making sure that your time is spent where it will create the most good. Your measurement of value is in the good that you create and the difference you are able to make in society or people's lives.

Some of you who are involved in spiritual counseling or healing wonder if it is spiritual to charge money for your services since your talent is a gift of spirit. Every talent that anyone has is a gift of spirit—a beautiful singing voice, a talent for mathematics, or an ability to write. The food a farmer grows is a gift from the land, and yet he or she is entitled to an exchange of money for the labor, time, and effort contributed to make the food available for people to buy. People pay you for the time, labor, and energy that is required of you to make your talents available to them. If you need money for your monthly expenses, your pay needs to be in the form of money. If you don't need money, you will still want to ask for something in return for your services, for others cannot complete the flow of energy if they don't give something back to you. It may be something as simple as appreciating your gift and using it to make a difference in their lives, or taking a few hours of their time to help you with something.

People value and honor my work.

Offer your work only to those who value it. If you work for an employer who doesn't value your work, it undermines your self-confidence. Before changing jobs, ask yourself whether you believe that you are a worthy, valuable person and that your services are important. Then look at what you are learning from being in your present situation. Once you understand what you are learning and the beliefs that created your situation, you will be able to find a job that honors you, and you may even find your current employer begins to treat you with more respect as well.

Even if you don't have an employer who honors you, you may have many clients or people you serve who do. Evaluate whether the good you are creating for people outweighs the fact that your work is not as valued by your company as you would like. It is important that those you offer your work to—clients, customers, businesses, or individuals—are able to use your services in some way to create higher good in their lives. If you are not receiving the pay you feel you deserve and you do not feel your job allows you to make a meaningful contribution, you will want to work with developing the quality of honoring and valuing your worth and time.

Offering your services or your work to those who don't value it can increase your doubts about your worth, cutting off the flow of your energy and thus your abundance. An artist decided to paint a portrait of one of her friends as a gift. She knew her friend was a very negative person who was usually complaining and unhappy. She felt that she could make a contribution to her friend, who thought of herself as unattractive, by painting her portrait. This painting would show her friend how radiant and beautiful she really was. It was quite an undertaking because she could paint only at night when her children were asleep. After several months, she finished and framed a beautiful portrait.

Her friend received the gift with her customary ingratitude. She thought the likeness was poor, and finally decided she wouldn't even hang it in her house. Everyone around her loved the painting and agreed it was a stunning likeness that truly brought out her beauty. The woman who painted it felt depressed for days and wasn't even sure she wanted to continue her artwork. Several months later, another friend called and wanted to pay her to do a portrait. She almost turned the job down, but since this friend liked her work so much, she decided to try again. She did the painting, and her friend was delighted.

Painting the first portrait gave her a valuable lesson because she had previously doubted the worth of her work. Her negative friend brought these doubts to the surface where she could work with them consciously and begin to release them. She also began to see that she did not need to be around negative people who did not believe in her life's work and took away her confidence. She vowed that she would paint only for those people who honored and valued her work. It was a turning point in her career, for with that new decision she began to get more satisfying work and bigger commissions. Perhaps you have offered a service that was unappreciated and you felt depreciated for a while afterward. That experience may have also been a turning point in your valuing of your work and yourself. Give your work only to those who will value and use it.

I *always give my best.*

Many of you choose to exchange your services rather than charge money for them. Once you have decided to exchange in this way, you will want to be clear about your expectations. Money was created so both parties could clearly agree upon an equal exchange. You may find it easier and clearer to receive money for your services rather than exchanging services directly. Bartering requires love, a willingness to make both parties winners, and a true desire to give to the other person in order to keep the energy flowing.

If you exchange goods or services directly with others, you want to find a way to establish agreements that work for both of you to create a clear, loving flow of energy between you. If you really can't use someone's services, it is better to say "no" than to accept someone's gift with resentment or a feeling that the exchange is unequal.

If you do accept an exchange, do so without reservation, giving your best and loving what you get in return. If you find afterward that the exchange doesn't feel quite fair, send the other person your thanks and love anyway, and know that by putting out your best you have kept your energy circulating. It will come back to you multiplied from another source if not from the person you gave it to. Do your best to make sure each of you benefits and is empowered by the exchange, and the integrity of your intent will multiply your abundance over and over.

PLAYSHEET

1 | What could you do right now to honor your worth more? For instance, you might offer your work to different people or increase what you charge for your services.

2 | Pick one of the things from above and create a picture of the circumstances you would like to experience. Make your picture as real and as detailed as possible.

CHAPTER 19

Joy and *Appreciation*

Money is magnetic; it flows and circulates. The more it flows and circulates, the richer a society is. You do not "create" money when you bring it into your life; you tap into a flow that is already there. When you create wealth you do not take from someone else; you become part of a flow of money. Let it circulate through you. Remember that the more money circulates, the wealthier everyone is, just as the more times inventory turns over, the more prosperous a store becomes. Prosperity comes when giving and receiving are flowing freely.

All the money I spend enriches society and comes back to me multiplied.

When you create money, you also spend it. You buy products, services, food, and things that give you joy. The more you circulate your money, the more you contribute to the wealth of your community. The more you feel good about sending out your money, the more magnetic your money becomes. When you pay your bills, do so with a generous and good feeling. Every time you pay a bill, you are adding to the circle of money; you are enriching society.

Imagine that there are many flows coming into you from the universe and each one offers a way money can come to you. Every time you have a doubt, every time you resent paying a bill, every time you do not believe in your prosperity, you close off one of those flows. Every time you send out your money with joy and love, you open another way for the universe to send you money. The next time you pay a bill, imagine that at least ten times more than the amount you pay out is coming back to you. See your money contributing to the prosperity of the person or institution you are paying.

All *the money I spend and earn brings me joy.*

Joy is an important attitude that will increase your prosperity. Learn to spend money, even small sums, in ways that bring you joy. When you have larger sums, you will know how to spend them with joy as well. You want your money to bring you happiness and joy. If you do not know how to spend a few dollars in a way that increases your happiness, it will be difficult to increase your happiness by spending thousands of dollars. Begin now to let your money bring you joy, and as the amount of money you have increases it will bring you more and more joy.

Think of a small sum of money that you could afford to spend right now in a different way than you normally would. Just for fun, think of at least five things you could spend this sum of money on, things that would bring you joy. These can be as outrageous and impractical as you want. Be as inventive as possible. One person thought of buying many small candles and putting them all over her house, then lighting them for a special meditation. Another thought of putting small bills in envelopes under windshield wipers of old cars, telling people how much they were appreciated. Pick one of your joyful ideas, and spend your money on it this week.

If you spend money without joy or love, out of obligation, resentment, worry, or with a feeling that you cannot afford what you buy, it will keep you out of the abundant flow of money. Observe how you spend money, and make a note of how you feel as you send it out. Note when the feeling is joyful and when it is not. Is there anything you are spending your money on right now that is an obligation and not a joy? Don't criticize yourself if you discover you are spending money out of obligation or without joy; simply focus on your spending that does bring you joy. As you spend money more frequently in ways that bring you joy, you will spend out of obligation less and less frequently.

What you buy gives a message to your subconscious about what you believe you deserve to have. Buy what you really want. Buy one good outfit that you feel wonderful wearing, rather than several less expensive ones that you don't really like. This tells your subconscious that you can have what you want, and it will immediately go about bringing you more. Rather than focusing on how much money you can save by buying something that doesn't excite you, buy something that will provide you with many alive moments of pleasure that engage your mind, your body, and your emotions. Of course, if you can buy something for less that you love just as much, do so—the cost isn't as important as your loving what you buy.

After buying something that means a lot to you, enjoy it. Play with it like a child who has just received a special toy he or she has been wanting. Appreciate what you have; become familiar with it; harmonize with it; learn all about it. Do this for a day, a week, or a month, until you've formed a complete relationship with it and put your energy into it. Harmonizing your energy with your new things completes the relationship with what you buy and helps you feel more fulfilled by them.

I *surround myself with things that reflect my aliveness and energy.*

Objects have energy. You feel the energy of the objects around you at a subtle level, so surround yourself with only those items you love and feel connected to. Broken or useless possessions clutter your energy; it is wise to keep the things around you in good repair so there is order and harmony about you.

One woman decided to have a garage sale and get rid of many unwanted possessions she and her husband had accumulated over many years. She went through every object in their house, and kept only those that she had a complete relationship with—things she appreciated, enjoyed, and used. After selling the rest of her possessions, she couldn't believe how light and energized she felt. It was as if a burden had been lifted—an energy burden. She had more energy and felt more positive than ever. Keep around you only those things you value and appreciate, and they will reflect that higher energy back to you.

Spend a moment right now to look around your home. Are you keeping objects that don't serve you anymore? Pick one of those objects and let it go—give it to a friend, recycle it, or sell it. You have just created the space for something even better to come into your life.

I *appreciate all that I am and all that I have.*

All of you have heard at one time or another, "Be appreciative; say thank you." What is the true value of gratitude? Gratitude acknowledges your power and ability to create.

It focuses your attention on what you have, and what you pay attention to increases. It is a constant reminder to yourself of how abundant the universe is and how you can trust its unending flow. Appreciation is a state of mind that magnetizes money and abundance to you.

Think of your subconscious as a small child. Have you ever noticed how children respond when you praise them, how much harder they try, how their faces light up with joy and their eyes sparkle? Every time you give thanks to yourself for something you have created, that little child within you lights up, sparkles, and wants to do even more for you. Every time you say, "That wasn't good enough; you could have done better," that little child closes down. Just like a child who is criticized, your subconscious loses confidence and courage. Appreciating yourself and thanking the universe motivates the child within you to create even more good in your life.

Appreciation is reflected in your attitude, and your attitude can either magnetize or repel money. You may have noticed that many successful businessmen write thank-you letters or send gifts to those who assist them. Thanking the universe for your abundance, either by mentally saying "thank you" or acknowledging your gratitude aloud, will multiply your prosperity.

I *appreciate myself.*
I give thanks for my wonderful life.

Every time you say "thank you" to yourself, you instill confidence in your ability to create what you want. Begin thanking the universe for every small thing that comes your way, appreciate how far you have come and all that you have already accomplished, and you will overcome your fears and doubts. Give thanks for all the things you take for granted— the place you live in, the friends who love you, the food on your table. Do not label what you have now as inadequate, but instead begin thanking the universe for it.

Every time you experience something you like, you can create even more of it in your life by using a process called "amplifying." For instance, say you have just experienced or received something you want more of. Stop for a moment and let the joy of having it grow stronger. Feel the satisfaction in your body, emotions, and mind. Then get quiet and imagine yourself amplifying that energy. Imagine those feelings are growing like a spiral of energy, starting in your heart and becoming the size of your body or even larger. By doing this you are making yourself magnetic to even more good things. Pretending that you are increasing your feelings of satisfaction and happiness, plus intending to have more good things appear in your life, is all that is required.

JOY AND APPRECIATION
PLAYSHEET

Joy:

1 | List several ways you might increase joy in your life.

2 | Pick one of these things. How might you use money as a tool to enhance your joy in this area?

Appreciation:

1 | List at least five things you accomplished last year that you feel good about. These can be minor or major accomplishments. You have probably accomplished even more than you realize or have given yourself credit for.

2 | Think of at least five things you are grateful for right now in your life. (One man made a mental list every night before he went to bed of everything he felt grateful for. His prosperity began to increase dramatically.)

3 | Think of at least three people to whom you would like to show your appreciation for their support right now. Be specific about what you would like to do, and then do it.

CHAPTER 20

Giving and Receiving

To create many flows of money in your life, learn to give and receive freely. You want to receive as well as give. Many of you love to give to others, yet it is harder to allow yourself to receive from them. You empower others by letting them give to you, for they then have the opportunity to demonstrate their abundance. People feel good about themselves when they give you something that you can use and appreciate. If no one could receive, no one would be able to give, which would block the flow of energy necessary to create abundance.

I am open to receive.

Do not see it as selfish for you to receive; see it as the completion of the circle of energy. The more you open to receive, the more you can give. Receive money from people, receive the form and substance of what they give you, and do so with warmth and graciousness. Imagine ten times the amount of money someone gives you coming back to them every time you receive money. As you envision success for other people, you increase your own magnetism to prosperity.

Be open to receiving with gratitude and grace. If you receive a check for ten dollars, thank the universe for it, rather than saying, "This is not enough." So many people receive money and say, "I don't know how I'm going to make this last, I wish I had received more." They take the amount and make it less, and less will come next time. If you receive money with an image of more coming, with a feeling of joy and thanks, you create more ways for the universe to give you prosperity.

Be open to receiving from any source that honors your integrity and be willing to get what you have asked for. Sometimes people look for hidden strings or for the flaws in what they are receiving. Imagine that you are looking for a used car. You decide to create a beautiful car at a very affordable price, a car that has very little mileage on it and is in excellent condition. You get clear on the essence of what you want and start magnetizing the car. Then one day you find a car that meets all of your conditions, and costs even less than you imagined. Rather than being pleased because it seems so perfect, some of you wonder if something is wrong! Trust your ability to create something ideal; affirm your power to create what you want. As you master the process of manifesting, you will often receive things that seem too good to be true, so enjoy what you create.

Once, as an experiment, a TV station hired a man to stand in the middle of New York City and hand out $20 bills. The results were amazing. Only one out of ten people would take the money. Reactions ranged from total avoidance of the man to "I'm not buying anything so don't bother me with your gimmick," to one man who took the money, looked it over and over, then shrugged his shoulders in bewilderment and walked away with it. Affirm that you will receive money from whatever source the universe uses to give it to you, and the universe will find more ways to give you money. Of course, if anyone is trying to buy your friendship, or the money is coming to you with strings attached that you don't like, do not accept it. Accept money from any source if people are giving it to you freely. The more easily you can receive, the more easily the universe can give to you.

Think of all the sources from which you allow money to come to you (e.g. your job, income from investments, your parents, scholarships). What other ways might you receive income? Include ways that seem improbable, such as anonymous checks, notification from the bank that you have more than you thought in your account, or an unexpected refund. Be as outrageous and imaginative as you can. Then ask yourself, "Am I willing to receive from new sources?" If you are, ask the universe to send you money through a new channel in the next several weeks. Be willing to acknowledge it when it comes, and congratulate yourself for creating new ways to receive abundance.

Sometimes it is easier to get what you want directly rather than first creating money for it. Think of something specific you want that you don't yet have. Instead of creating the money for it, decide that you will focus on having it and letting it come in any way possible. Then follow your inner guidance. Suppose that you want a bicycle. As you keep focusing on the bicycle, you may find that one of your friends, or someone they know, will lend you a bicycle or ask you to store his while he is away. Rather than first having to attract the money and then the object, it is sometimes faster to get the object directly.

Everything I give to others is a gift to myself. As I give I receive.

Giving is an important part of receiving. The way you give to others is the way the universe will give to you. Giving money or other things is truly a gift to yourself, for it creates a circulation of energy in your life, and the more energy circulates the wealthier you are. There was a man who liked to flip coins into the street where little children would find them. He knew that they would feel it was their lucky day, that money had dropped out of the clear blue sky. Later on, he became a real estate developer. When he wanted investment money for the projects he had put together, the money came easily, "out of the clear blue sky," as if it was a lucky find.

It is a law of the universe that to get something you need to give something. If there is something you want, you can ask yourself, "What do I need to give to get it?" Everything has a price. If you want money, the price may be action, right attitude, or a plan. There is always something you can do to have what you want. If you want more money, you need to give those things in your life that will bring you money. That includes your talents, skills, time, and energy.

If you are feeling a lack of abundance in your life, think of someone you can give something to. Giving to others who are appreciative and can use your gifts can bring you some of the most wonderful feelings in the world. Giving affirms your abundance and helps you feel prosperous. Giving makes you strong. Think of something you could give to someone you know that would help him or her right now. Make a point of doing it, and you will find the universe will give to you as well.

E*very gift I give serves*
and empowers other people.

While you want to give freely and generously to people, you also want to give to people in a way that truly serves their higher good. When you give money to people, be clear that you are giving money to create their prosperity, not to bail them out of a recurring situation. Give to people who will use your money and gifts to create positive changes in their lives. When you see people putting together concrete plans and going out into the world, coming from their true essence, that is the time to support them. Give in order to help people achieve their higher purposes and paths.

When people are constantly in need, always creating lack, your giving may just keep bailing them out and preventing them from making their lives work. People create lack in their lives to learn certain lessons. If you find yourself giving people money or things but their lives aren't improving, it may be time to reexamine your giving. You may be taking away the growth they are gaining from experiencing their lack.

Perhaps someone seeming desperate once asked you for money, and you said, "No." Then he pulled himself through, getting a job, or making his life work better. Many times people create a sense of lack or scarcity to motivate themselves to make changes in their lives. "Saving" people from their crises may only create dependency, and you may find them creating the same situation over and over.

Helping people get in touch with their inner strengths or teaching them problem-solving skills usually makes more of a contribution to their lives than giving them money. Work with them to help them discover ways to solve their problems. This helps them become stronger and gain more control of their lives. You empower others when you teach them a new method, skill, or tool that they can learn and use for the rest of their lives.

If you have people in your life who seem to be financially needy and you feel obligated to bail them out, remember that you are affirming that they aren't strong. They have the same power within them to create abundance as you do. Help them discover that power and you will have given them one of the greatest gifts of all—self-sufficiency. Of course, there are people for whom the gift of a meal, a place to sleep, or clothes to wear is not "saving" them but giving them the help they need at a critical time so that they can keep on growing. You will know the difference by the feeling in your heart; if you are truly empowering people you will feel uplifted and joyful from your giving.

Everything I give others honors and acknowledges their worth.

Give what is joyful to give; do not give money if you feel obligated or forced to give it. Any heavy feelings are signs that such giving is not for the highest good of that person. Some parents feel obligated to continue helping their children even after they are grown and could be on their own. There may come a time when you need to say "no" to a request for money; your "no" comes from a place of greater love than any resentful "yes" could.

One man had a brother who was constantly unable to pay his rent. He kept giving his brother rent money, but nothing seemed to change. Finally, he refused to give his brother money, knowing that he had to learn to solve this basic problem. He realized that just giving him money wouldn't teach him how to take care of himself. He worked with his brother to help him discover what he wanted to do for a living, and brought him books on how to get a new job.

Shortly thereafter, the brother got a job that paid enough to cover his rent. He started going to night school to learn how to operate a computer, since he had discovered that he loved working with them. There weren't enough computers at school to allow him to practice as much as he wanted, so he asked his brother if he could borrow money to buy his own computer. The man did make the loan, because the computer would help his brother become more prosperous. Later, the brother began his own computer business and became quite successful.

Remember to give others what they wish to receive. Not all gifts are appropriate. When someone gives a small pet to a child it may require much care and attention from a parent who does not have the time. Make sure your gift is in a form that is acceptable to the recipient, and something he or she can truly use. Give freely, but also give those things that truly serve the person you are giving to.

I *give generously to myself.*

Learning to give to yourself is important in maintaining the flow of abundance. If you cannot give to yourself, there will be a block in the flow, and eventually you will feel it. For instance, healers may burn themselves out if they are always giving to others but are unable to give themselves the time they need to feel nurtured and recharge their energy. You may start experiencing lack, then have to put extraordinary amounts of time and energy into yourself. Or, you may feel depleted on an energy level from your work and lose your enthusiasm for what you are doing.

Often when people give, they do not completely release what they have given. Give your gifts without strings. If you give a gift to someone, release it. When you are attached to what you give, you block the flow of more into your life. If you give away your old clothes and you keep thinking how you could still use them, wishing you hadn't given them away, you will be blocking the arrival of new ones, for you haven't truly released the old. Whenever you give, be clear that you are giving freely, for the more freely you give, the more easily you will attract money.

Money comes when you put your attention into what you are giving to the world rather than thinking only of the money your work will bring you. Your willingness to do your best work is the greatest gift you give your employer or clients. Work with a spirit of cooperation and love. Your willingness to put your energy and commitment behind your work will gain you more money than cutting corners, not believing in what you are doing, resisting your work, or doing just enough to get by.

An artist was worried that he wouldn't make enough money from his art work to support himself. He judged every opportunity that came along by how much money it cost or would make him. He turned down several opportunities that looked inviting but didn't appear to offer enough money. He was constantly short of money. An artist friend of his, on the other hand, did all he could to be a good artist. He took classes, followed his inner urges and joy, and gave his best. Rather than paying attention to the money his activities brought, he asked, "How can I best serve the people who are coming to see my work? What can I give them? Would I love to take this opportunity? What can I do to be the best possible artist?"

Eventually his work became well known and he made a very comfortable living. His friend, who was always thinking of money rather than serving people, ended up making little money, and his work didn't get out to the world. Evaluate your opportunities by taking into account whether they contribute to others, are on your path, and bring you joy. You create money by using your special skills and talents, and by doing your best at whatever you do.

I *serve others to the best of my ability*
in all I say and do.

People who serve others to the best of their ability have lives filled with abundance and joy. Service means putting yourself in other people's shoes and giving them the best you can, be they clients, employers, co-workers, friends, or loved ones. When you show your best face to the world and come from your highest level of integrity, you are serving others. You do not need to be a leader, world famous, or accomplish great deeds to make an important contribution to humanity. If your work is done with intention, consciousness, and love, you are giving the most valuable contribution of all— you are adding light to the world.

There was a salesman whose sales had begun dropping off, and he couldn't understand why. He still loved what he was doing; he believed in the product he was selling and felt that he was accomplishing his higher purpose. One day in talking to a friend he came to the realization that he was no longer focusing on serving and giving to people, but had begun to think of them only in terms of what they could give him. He was not seeing them as people he served but instead as numbers that put money into his pocket. He had become so focused on making money that he had forgotten he was in the business of serving people. He changed his ways and put his attention on how he could best serve each person, regardless of whether he made a sale. He spent time getting to know his customers, learning of their wants, and sincerely trying to help them. He gave freely of his love, time, and energy. His sales increased dramatically.

The more you think about serving others, the greater and more fulfilling your work will be. As you focus on how your work could give light and joy to other people, you will find that it brings light and joy to you as well. Service is giving others the best you know how to give. It means that you are efficient, considerate, and conscious when you go about your work. It means you work with an attitude of joy, harmony, and cooperation with those about you. Service will always come back to you many times over as increased prosperity.

The greatest gift you give others is the example of your own life working.

GIVING AND RECEIVING
PLAYSHEET

Receiving:

1 | List as many things as you can think of that you would like to receive. Describe the form as specifically as you can if you know what it is.

2 | Go over each item. Ask yourself if you are truly willing to receive it? Are there differences in your answers for different items?

3 | Take something you feel most open to receive. Observe what the feeling "open to receive" is like. Does it have a feeling in your body? In your emotions or thoughts?

4 | Take something you don't feel as open to receive from your list above. Remembering how it felt to be open to receive, play with your thoughts, feelings, and physical sensations until you feel more open to receive this thing.

Giving:

1 | Is there someone you are thinking of giving something to? Reflect carefully. Are you giving to his or her need, or to his or her prosperity?

2 | If you are not feeling abundant right now in your life, is there something you could give to another person to demonstrate your belief in your prosperity? If there is, give it.

CHAPTER 21

Clarity and Harmony

If you want money to flow, be clear and truthful with yourself about what you want in exchange for your efforts and time. This means having clear agreements with other people about what you want from them and what you are willing to give them. If you are seeking smoothness and harmony in your personal and business financial dealings, you will want to be clear about your expectations and assumptions.

I experience clarity and harmony in all my energy exchanges.

If you are to be satisfied and happy with the outcome of your energy exchanges or financial transactions, be definite from the beginning about commitments, agreements, the time involved, effort to be expended, duties to be performed, and the rate of return. When you invest your money in something—be it a savings account, new business, house, real estate, stocks, or bonds—be clear about what you expect to get out of it financially. For instance, when you open a savings account, you and the bank have a clear agreement about how your rate of return is calculated, which eliminates disappointment and conflict.

People sign contracts to make sure that both parties agree on the terms and that there are no unspoken or hidden expectations. Often the process of coming to agreement generates the clarity between people that promotes love and harmony rather than conflict or struggle. Once you have a good working agreement there is rarely a problem. Think of a contract as an opportunity to create clarity between you and another person. Read it carefully and reflect on the terms. Are the terms agreeable to you? Do they reflect your intent?

It is important to have terms and agreements that serve your rights and interests as well as serving the other person. Don't be afraid to ask for clarification or alteration of terms you don't understand or disagree with before you sign. Whenever you enter into exchanges with others, whether or not contracts are involved, be clear about what your agreements are. The clearer you are the more harmony and light you put into your life. Your clarity is a gift to everyone in your life.

It is not practical to sign contracts with your friends about your day-to-day interactions, but you can bring the same clarity into your unspoken arrangements. Think of a friend. What unspoken agreements exist between you about your commitments to each other? For instance, how often are you expected to keep in contact? Are you expected to be available during a crisis? Do you lend each other money? You have many unspoken agreements with people in your life, granting them certain rights and privileges with your time and energy. When you and your friends disagree on the terms, or when you are unclear about what you are willing to give, conflicts arise. In the agreements you just thought about, are there any areas where you are not clear about your agreements? Take a moment now to bring clarity to those areas, deciding what you are willing to give and how you would like your agreements to be.

I *feel good about all the money I spend.*

You also have agreements with yourself. For instance, you have agreements with yourself about the way you allow yourself to spend money. What things are all right to spend on? How much money do you allow yourself to spend for certain things? For instance, do you say, "I have agreed that it is all right to spend money on groceries, however much it costs to fix good meals, as often as I want them. I have agreed not to spend money on an expensive outfit unless I want it for a specific event, and the event must be a fairly important one. If for some reason I buy some expensive clothing that is not for an important event, it must be something that can be worn frequently, so that the cost per wearing makes it inexpensive."

Take a moment to reflect on some of your agreements with yourself about what it is all right to spend money on. You will be surprised at how many internal guidelines you have set for yourself about money (and other areas of your life as well). You usually know when you have violated one of your agreements, for when you have, you feel guilty about spending money.

Make agreements with yourself about money that work to create joy, abundance, and clarity for you. If you are constantly feeling guilty about spending money, review the agreements you have made with yourself and think about changing them, for they are not working for you. You will want to examine whether your agreements are good ones, or if they are based on other people's values—those of your parents, society, or friends. Make agreements about money that work for you.

Think of a time you spent money and felt guilty afterward. What agreement about money did you violate? Is that a good agreement to have in your life? Does following that agreement help you love yourself? For instance, one woman always felt guilty when she bought something beautiful, and realized she had an agreement that it was all right to buy things that had a practical use, but not all right to buy things such as artwork and paintings just for the beauty they contributed to her environment. She made a new agreement with herself that spending a certain amount of money on beautiful, decorative objects was acceptable. Thereafter, as long as she stayed within her agreed-upon budget, she felt good about buying decorative items for her home.

I *am always being guided to the higher solution.*

A lack of clear agreements about money can create conflicts between people, even two people who love each other. If one person has the agreement with himself or herself that it is all right to spend unlimited money on food, and does so, but the other person has the self-agreement to spend only a limited amount on food, there is potential for conflict. Each person is putting a different value on the food. Rather than taking the time to look at their agreements about money, discussing them calmly and lovingly, most people get into power struggles when these kinds of issues arise.

To many people money represents power, and being right about money represents having or gaining power. Money conflicts usually revolve around power struggles. Power may be the real issue when somebody owes you money and isn't paying it back, when you don't agree with your loved ones on how to spend money, or when you are not getting paid what you think you are worth.

If you find that money issues are causing disagreements or are creating distance between you and another person, you can work with love to change the situation. First, get quiet and go within. You may notice that you feel an uncomfortable energy in your stomach or right around the lower diaphragm. This indicates that you are struggling over who is right and who will win the power struggle. There is no way to win when you are fighting at this level.

I *listen to the wisdom of my heart.*

To change the situation, work at an energy level. You can start by going to your heart and releasing your anger and hurt. Send the other person your love. Release the need to be right or to have your way. You are not giving up your values or sacrificing your ideals. You are simply taking the energy out of your solar plexus (sometimes called the "power center") and moving it into your heart, where all true solutions are found.

Keep working with this until you can feel love and forgiveness for the other person. It may take several days or even longer before you can let go of anger and begin to have loving feelings. In the interim, do not take any action; don't argue, call, or do anything other than clean up the energy between you by sending the other person love. At some point you will feel a shift; you will feel love. Tell the other person mentally that you refuse to get into a power struggle. You are taking an "I win–you lose" situation and making it into a "we both win" situation.

When you go to your heart for answers, you open the doors for a new solution, a higher answer, to appear. Let this difficult situation go, and you will find new ideas coming to you. People will meet you halfway, for they will feel the change in your energy and make shifts themselves. Bombard people with thoughts of love and you can produce miraculous changes in any situation.

If someone owes you money, release the money and send the person love. Trust that the money will come from somewhere else, or even from that person once you truly release your attachment to having it. Refusal to pay debts is often a withholding of love, turning the relationship into a power struggle. If you refuse to join in this struggle and send love instead, you create a shift. Once you shift your energy, the other person cannot help but shift his or her energy as well.

Take the time to review your agreements, values, and beliefs about money in any area where you have financial conflict. The other party is bringing up an issue that is important for you to look at. What are you defending? You often defend most vigorously those beliefs and values you aren't really sure about, for when you are clear about your beliefs you rarely feel the need to defend them.

Think of a recent disagreement you had about money. What value or belief of yours was in question? What value or belief was the other person defending? Is there anything helpful about his or her belief, a new thought or place of clarity, that you might want to consider having for yourself? Are there parts of your beliefs or agreements that aren't working for you that you might benefit by letting go of? Your higher self wants you to look at your beliefs, values, and agreements or this situation would not have occurred.

Conflict can also come from a belief in scarcity, the idea that there is not enough for everyone. Think of a recent disagreement or small conflict you had about money. Was fear of not having enough partly responsible for your disagreement? If you believed that the universe was truly abundant and you could have whatever you wanted, would this conflict still have arisen? Make sure that you are not operating out of fear that there is not enough in the universe for both of you.

*I always look for ways
to make the other person a winner;
as I help others win, I win as well.*

There is always a way for both people to win. If it still appears to you that for one of you to win the other has to lose, you haven't arrived at the higher solution yet. The higher solution will always be a win for both people, with both their higher goals being met. To find this higher solution, first ask yourself, "What are the real issues? What is really important for me to have?" Question yourself honestly about what you need to meet your goals. Often you are fighting about one thing when the issue is something else entirely. Then, work together to find a solution.

Don't assume that the other person is against you; instead enlist him or her in finding a solution with you for the common problem you share. Always assume that there is a solution that will satisfy both of you, even if you haven't found it yet. Make it your goal to find a way for the other person to come out a winner, and you will make it possible for yourself to come out a winner as well.

It is time for new forms to emerge, for many of the old ways no longer work. It is your challenge to find new ways. Be willing to be open and flexible, to trust that there is a higher way. As it emerges through your love and intent, you will present mankind with the gifts of new solutions to old problems.

CLARITY AND HARMONY
PLAYSHEET

1 | What agreements have you made with yourself about spending? Make a list of things you spend money on, and after each thing, write the guidelines you follow when spending money on this item. (Such as how much money is allowed for these things or how often can you buy them?)

2 | Relax and get quiet for a moment. Review the agreements you have just written. What changes could you make in these agreements that would allow you to feel more abundant? Rewrite your agreements.

CHAPTER 22

Having Money

Money is neither good nor bad; it is energy. It is the way money is used that determines whether or not it is a positive energy that will benefit you and others. If you come from the highest level of integrity with your money, if you make it in ways that benefit people, through shifting their consciousness, or through serving and making a contribution, by giving your best, honoring others, and putting attention and consciousness into what you do, you are making a contribution to mankind and to yourself. When you use money in ways that serve your higher purpose and bring you and others joy, you are creating money of light. The more money is made and spent with integrity and light, the more it becomes a force of light for everyone.

I *have abundance in every area of my life.*

True abundance is having all you need to do your life's work—the tools, resources, living environment, and to live a life filled with joy and aliveness. Abundance is not an extravagant, glamorous style of living maintained purely to impress others or one that does not support your true aliveness and life's work. Part of the essence of spirituality is the belief in true abundance—of time, love, and energy. You teach others by setting an example. It may be hard, if not impossible, to help others lead abundant lives if you do not have a feeling of abundance about your own life. You do not want living at a survival level and experiencing lack to be the examples you set. When you have the right amount of money and money works in your life, people will learn about abundance by your example.

Most war and strife come from a belief in scarcity. People who believe in scarcity also try to squeeze more and more out of nature, wasting the planet's resources. If you want to contribute to planetary peace, you can start by believing in abundance for yourself and others. As society begins to believe that there can be abundance for everyone, new discoveries will be made that will provide unlimited energy and resources that do not pollute or deplete the earth, and there will be fewer reasons for war. There truly is the potential for abundance for everyone on the planet. If mankind believed in abundance for all, it could be created. Start by believing that it is possible for everyone to have abundance.

M*y prosperity prospers others.*

It is all right to have money. Some of you feel guilty about having money, especially when you look around and see others living in lack. Some people learn and grow as much by having a totally materialistic focus as others do by living in poverty. It is not more spiritual to be poor, nor is it better to be rich. If you are worried that it is not spiritual to have money, examine the times in your life when you had money, even if it was just a small amount. Remember how you used your money. You may have been able to help those around you even more.

When you felt abundant, you probably felt generous and able to support others in their abundance.

The people who are clearest about money are not usually those who have large sums of money, or those who have none, but those who have just the right amount for them. People who have just the right amount are not burdened by too many possessions; their possessions serve them. They do not spend time and energy that would be best spent creating their life's work to acquire or take care of material things. Having too much money can take you off your path if you must spend a lot of time taking care of it. Not having enough money can also take you off your path if it requires a lot of your time and energy just to survive. It is important for you to have enough money to live on. If you do not have enough, if you spend most of your time worrying about your rent and food, your time and energy are not available to do the greater work you came here to do.

Think of being "rich" as having enough wealth to carry out your life's work. You may not need many material possessions to have "enough." For instance, your life purpose may be to work with nature. You may live in a log cabin, spend little money, and still have all the natural resources you need to carry out your purpose. In that case, you would be rich. What is important is having enough money to do the work you came to do, and not having so much that it keeps you from the work you came to do. Having enough money means being able to put your vision into action, to transform the energy around you into a higher order. Some people may need many material things to accomplish their life purpose. They may need to work with a group of people who will only listen to and respect them if they have an appearance of wealth and power.

Material possessions may provide some with a spiritual experience, teaching them what they need to learn in this lifetime, just as not having money may be a great teacher for others. Some people gain great freedom and growth from having money; some people gain freedom and growth from not having money.

How much money people need is an individual matter; do not judge others for what they have or do not have. Some people may be amassing fortunes that will later be used for the good of mankind, even if at present they don't plan on using their money this way and aren't on a spiritual path. You cannot know the larger purpose of anyone's path. It is good to measure people's success not by how much money they make or have, but by the degree to which they are fulfilling their life purpose, are happy about their lives, have the right amount of money, and believe in themselves.

Everyone's success contributes
to my success.

As you become more prosperous yourself, it is likely that you will be around prosperous people. As you think in terms of prosperity, your vibration begins to change and you attract other people who think in terms of abundance as well. Do not feel jealous or threatened by someone who is successful. Realize that if you are close to a person who is succeeding, you are beginning to have that same vibration of success yourself. Begin now to believe that everyone's success means even more success for you. If everyone around you begins to succeed, then you are surrounded with the vibration of success and your success will grow even faster. When you hear of other people's good fortune, appreciate their success, knowing that it affirms the abundance that is available for you as well.

Many of you think that you have to get your work out to a large number of people or be number one in your field to truly be successful. It is not wrong to feel competitive if that feeling helps you do your best at your job; but don't feel that others who succeed in what you are doing can take away from your success. There is an unlimited supply of success. Every person in the world can be successful. Realize that you have your special place, and what you are here to do is in some way special and unique, no matter how many people are doing similar things. Is there a person or company you are competing with? Are you worried that their success might mean a loss to you? Take a moment to picture them succeeding beyond your wildest dreams. Then, imagine a reason why their success will be beneficial to you.

Know that there is no one else in the world who is going to do your work exactly as you do it. Even if it appears that others are doing the same work, they are probably reaching a different group of people, or reaching the same group in a different way. It is better to focus on living up to your potential. Are you putting the wants of people you serve first? Are you following your inner messages? As you do, you will shine. You will have all the business and abundance you want. Enjoy the process of getting your work out, not just to strive for recognition and fame. Let it be all right not to be "number one," have the most clients, make the most money, or think you must do it all yourself.

Do not worry about someone else taking away your idea, or doing what you are doing better than you are. As long as you do the best you know how and put out the finest quality product or service you can offer, you will be richly rewarded. It doesn't matter what other people do. Even if someone is claiming the credit right now for your good work, don't stop putting out quality work. You will be rewarded eventually. As with the tortoise and the hare, the one who works consistently and steadily, doing a good job all the time, will have more abundance and make a greater mark in the world than the person who takes shortcuts to beat everyone else out.

If you are competing with other job applicants for a job, or other businesses for a client, or wanting to get a grant or funding, do not view yourself as competing with others. If it is for your highest good to get the money, client, or job, you will. Always do your best in your grant applications, job interviews, or sales presentations; write or go to only those people your inner messages direct you to, and you will find your money or job. If you get it, do not worry that you have taken something away from someone else.

The universe is perfect and abundant, and others will receive exactly what is best for them. You cannot take away from others. Your opportunities are meant for you, and those that aren't for you will be given to others. If you are "competing" for anything right now—a job, funding, a loan, a scholarship, or an apartment—see if you can let go of your worry and trust that the best outcome will occur for all of you. Trust that what is meant to be yours will be yours; the universe is always working to bring your higher good to you.

Don't view your co-workers or those around you as competitors; see them as friends. Cooperation will get you much further than competition. One man who worked for a company wanted to be the vice president in a short period of time. He went around telling everyone of his ambitions, often praising his own work. He undermined the work of other employees so that his own work would appear better, and tried to take the credit himself for work that others had done. Another man in the same company simply wanted to do the best job he could. He was constantly thinking of his fellow employees, took on extra jobs, helped his boss out whenever he could, and performed the job he was hired for with attention and love. The first man was not promoted and quit in anger with many grievances against the company that "just couldn't appreciate him." The second man went on to become vice president.

I *send others thoughts of their increased prosperity.*

When you think of others and yourself, have thoughts of riches, prosperity, success, and goodness. Having such thoughts helps make them come true. Let your thoughts about everyone be of their increased good. Picture everyone as successful. Sometimes people bring financial hardship to themselves by dwelling on other people's financial difficulties, for what you focus on is what you draw to yourself. Rather than talking about how hard life is for people, send them compassion and light; see them getting out of their difficult situations and experiencing abundance. The positive pictures and love you send out will come back to you many times over.

One storekeeper increased his business dramatically by sending love and envisioning success for everyone who came into his store. People were magnetically drawn to his shop. If you hear friends complaining of lack, remind them of what they do have. When you are around people who talk of financial problems, see if you can change the subject or help them appreciate the abundance they have already created.

You may be hoping that your wealth will come from winning a lottery. To win, be ready to receive the money. While many of you hope to win, you don't truly expect to win. People who win are committed to winning, and have dealt with their beliefs that say getting money this way is too easy, or too good to be true. Even more importantly, if winning the money would stop you from doing your life's work, your higher self will keep you from winning. Winning a large sum of money can create more challenges than you think. It is important to have the right amount of money, and if a huge windfall would put your life out of balance, your higher self will most probably keep it from you.

Depending on how prepared you are to have a large windfall, many things in your life will change. Getting money gradually, at a pace you can adjust to, is a gift. You can get used to handling a larger energy flow in a balanced, stable way. You have the time to try out various actions before large sums are involved. If you aren't prepared to handle a larger amount and you do get it, your higher self may find many ways for you to let go of it. Many people who have won or inherited large sums have also lost or spent them in just a few years; their own energy and the larger sum of money weren't in harmony. Those who do keep their windfalls often keep the same jobs and homes and bank the money, slowly getting used to the increased amount.

Play lotteries if you grow from the process. For many people lotteries provide an opportunity to visualize themselves as abundant, and that picture helps them draw in abundance in other ways. Every time they buy lottery tickets they feel the possible joy of winning, and bring that feeling into their lives. That may be precisely the feeling their souls want them to develop. You can create the same experience by visualizing your success, imagining having what you want, and making the picture as real and vivid as possible.

M*y money is a source of good
for myself and others.*

When you have money, see your money as a source of good; see it as potential to create higher purpose that has yet to be converted into substance and form. Keep picturing all your money in the bank or in your wallet as money that is awaiting your command to go out and create good for you and others. Appreciate your abundance and realize that you have learned to tap in to the unlimited abundance of the universe. Your money is awaiting the opportunity to bring you good, to improve your life and the lives of others.

PLAYSHEET

1 | How much spending money would you like to have for pure play and enjoyment?

2 | How much money would you like to have in your savings account?

3 | What would you like your net worth to be?

4 | What annual income would you like?

5 | What do you want money for in the next year or two? List as many things as you can think of.

6 | Choose one item from your answer to question 5 that stands out the most for you and complete the following:

a. List at least three ways that this item will serve your higher good.

b. List at least three ways that your having this item will serve the higher good of others.

CHAPTER 23

Savings: Affirming Your Abundance

There is great value, even if you are in debt, in using some of your money to create savings. Savings are fluid, accessible money, easily redeemable cash. Savings are a contribution to the flow of money in society, for money that is saved can be circulated to create more wealth. Your money can be used many times while it is "sitting" in a savings account. That is the reason you receive interest; it is payment for the wealth your money is creating for others as well as yourself. Savings give you resources that allow you to be self-sufficient. Savings are also a positive affirmation that you have more than you need at the moment. As you feel abundant, you become magnetic to even more money.

Money you save is useable energy that is immediately available when you want it. If you have stored money, you are less likely to be influenced by the ebb in the normal ebb-and-flow cycle. Nature uses this principle; just observe squirrels storing their nuts for the winter, or bears hibernating to save their energy. You can take advantage of opportunities when you have money saved. Think of your savings as your "expanding possibilities account" that will allow you more choices and more freedom. Savings allow you to have greater control over the timing of your purchases. Some things you may want may require a large sum of money to acquire. By having savings available you can get what you want when you want it.

M*y savings act as a magnet to draw more money.*

Some of you may think that savings indicate your lack of trust in your ability to create money when you want it. Let us look at savings in a different way. You are always storing and saving money. Unless you instantly spend it, when you receive a sum of money for your services you are saving money. Since you are already practicing saving money between the time you receive it and the time you spend it, all you need to do is save a larger amount than normal between receiving and spending. The money you save acts as a "money magnet" to attract more money. The larger your savings, the larger your magnet.

What is the most money you have ever had stored up before you spent it? What is the largest amount of savings you have ever had? Many people, when they come close to having saved more money than they ever had in the past, begin to spend it. To increase your savings, increase the amount of money you allow yourself to have left over after your expenditures. Observe yourself when you come close to your past limit, and create the intent to break through this savings "barrier." By simply becoming aware of your limit you are halfway to breaking through.

You can create a surplus in the flow as it goes through you if you consciously allow a larger and larger sum to accumulate before you spend it. You don't need a fortune to start a savings account. A little bit of money put away every month can become a sizable amount of cash in five or ten years. The greatest benefit of saving money is that it allows you to get used to a larger and larger flow of money and the energy it represents, which is what you are asking for if you want increased abundance.

Many of you want to reach a level of mastery with money and abundance where you will be able to manifest whatever you need when you need it. This may mean getting things without needing money for them, or learning to attract large sums of money instantly for those larger-than-normal purchases. To do this you will want to become a master at attracting a steady flow (to cover your monthly expenses) and also be able to attract large surges in the flow (to handle big purchases). If you are creating what you want from moment to moment, you will need to be able to adjust your energy to constantly varying levels of flow. Most people are used to only a certain range and a fairly consistent energy flow; they allow their monthly income to be no less and no greater than a certain amount.

Saving money will help you get comfortable with a greater and greater amount of energy so that you will be able to handle a larger flow. Once you master a new level of flow and are comfortable with a greater surplus, the amounts required for larger purchases will be fairly easy for you to create. You may not even need to touch the money you have saved. Your savings can act as a safety net for the times that you aren't as consistently magnetic to money as you would like to be.

I *am financially independent and free.*

Many of you wish you could be free every day to do what you want, without concern for money. You want financial freedom. There are several ways to create that reality. One is to create ways that what you love to do can bring you money, turning what you do for fun and relaxation into your source of prosperity. You can also gain greater and greater skill in drawing to you what you need when you need it. Another approach is to have enough money so that you can live off the interest. Any method will work; decide which way will satisfy the essence of what you want and then begin to master the skills necessary to create it.

In the meantime, as you are learning these skills, starting to save will help you become familiar with the energy of the greater flow of money and abundance you are seeking. It will help you accumulate enough energy to make a big change in your life or purchase something larger than normal that is really important to you.

If you don't believe you can have a surplus, if you believe yourself to be poor, you will create that as your reality whether you have a small or large sum of money. Begin by believing that you deserve abundance, and use your savings as an affirmation that there is more abundance for you than you require at this moment. When you think of the money you have saved, think of how you are going to use it. That will help you attract more money to put into your savings.

Think of how much you would like in your savings; imagine it as vividly as you can. Imagine the balance you would like. Envision yourself putting money into your account. Feel the joy you will have when you look at the balance. Don't think of it as saving for a calamity or disaster; if you do, you will keep creating emergencies that require your savings. Picture your savings as your wealth account. View it as money that is teaching you how to handle a larger and larger flow of prosperity.

All my money is energy
awaiting my command
to create good in my life.

Make sure that when you take your money out of savings you spend it for something special, something you have a great desire for. This charges your money with aliveness, and makes all of the money you have more magnetic. Ask, "How can I use my savings to serve my higher purpose?"

One of the best uses of your savings is empowering your life's work. You will discover that those who become wealthy put their extra money into their dreams, investing in themselves before they invest in areas they know little about. Spend money on those things that help you get your work out into the world, be they books or classes, equipment, the right clothes for your job, or remodeling your house to make room for an office or place to do your work. Using your money to create your life's work will draw to you even more money. If you have all you need for your life's work, you may want to continue storing your money until the right use for it appears.

As you create an excess of money, there are many ways to store it. You can keep it liquid and immediately accessible, such as in a savings account, or you can put it into investments that are less liquid. If you are thinking about investing ask, "Is it part of my life's path and the highest use of my time to be navigating the flows of this particular investment?" Savings-type of investments involve the least expenditure of your time and energy and require the least amount of watching and care.

Storing your money in investments other than savings-type investments will involve the use of your time to monitor them. You will need certain skills. Perhaps you will need to learn more about the stock market, gather information, make contacts, and monitor the daily news. Decide how you want to spend your time. If you invest your money in real estate, you will want to learn what property makes a good investment.

Don't just turn your money over to others, especially if they don't have prosperity consciousness. If you give responsibility for your investments to other people, make sure they have a good understanding of what they are doing and that you have the ability to monitor and evaluate their performance according to your own criteria. It is your money, your energy that is being stored, and you want to keep a certain watchfulness so that your investments stay connected to your energy. How you store your money will depend on who you are, what you like to do, and how you like to spend your time.

All my money is working for me to increase my abundance, joy, and aliveness.

Wherever you store your money, stay conscious of what is being done with it and check on it fairly frequently. Don't be unconscious of where your money is stored. You don't want your money held in a place that doesn't match your energy. If you open a savings account or invest in any project, make sure the people working with your money have a good business background and a knowledge of the spiritual and human-made principles of money. People without this knowledge won't be able to make good investments for you, no matter how good their ideas are. Make sure their beliefs and thoughts about money are as much in alignment with yours as possible. Are you treated well where you store your money? Does the energy there feel right to you? Do the people who handle your investments have similar standards of integrity and a similar philosophy to yours, such as making every party come out a winner? All this is important if you want your money to do well.

If you are spending a lot of time managing your investments, be certain that this is your highest joy and your life's work. It is often best to put your excess money in a safe storage place that doesn't require too much of your energy, and spend your time and money doing your life's work. Ultimately, time and money spent doing your life's work will bring you a far greater return. Find a balance between putting enough of your energy into your investments so that they reflect your energy and putting time into your life's work and contribution to humanity. Think about where you want to be in five or ten years, and invest your money in a way that it becomes a part of your plan to get there.

If you want to invest in other people's businesses or financially fund their life's work, be aware that this is a business in itself. Many people who have arrived at this level of abundance find that properly evaluating others' projects can become a full-time undertaking. It may be that this is your life's work. It is best to invest in projects that are closely aligned with who you are, rather than investing in projects you don't understand. Invest your money in the things you know about—your own business or your area of expertise. The more connected you are with the ideas that your money is serving, the better.

As you gain financial independence, your greatest challenge will be finding the highest use of your money and ways of investing it that create the greatest amount of change and good on the planet. You have many choices about what you can invest in. There are many good investments that honor the earth, help humanity, and use your money to create good. Hold each investment up to your soul's light, not only to determine its potential return, but to evaluate its potential to increase light for humanity and the planet. Make sure you know what your money will be used for, and that you believe in those things. If no appropriate projects have appeared for you to invest in, then continue to store your money in a place you feel good about until the right opportunity appears.

I *choose to live an abundant life.*

Those who achieve great wealth and service do not usually do so overnight. They focus on what they love to do, and almost always invest their money in their own work, not in investments they aren't familiar with. They are so absorbed in their work that they pursue it consistently and steadily over a number of years, even though what they started doing is not always the line of work they stay in. They gain much knowledge and experience, seeking to educate and expand themselves whenever the opportunity presents itself. Their dedication to their life's work brings them financial prosperity.

Those who do not make money or experience abundance are usually those who think they have to work at jobs they don't like until they have enough money saved to do work they like. They may try get-rich-quick investments that seem too good to be true and usually are. The path to lasting wealth and abundance is to do your life's work, follow the spiritual laws of money, work with energy and magnetism before you take action, and live a life that is loving and joyful to you.

We have covered in this book all the skills you will need to become a master of manifesting. As with any skill, mastery takes practice. As you practice you will learn much about yourself and the subtleties of working with energy. Enjoy your success when you create something, even a small thing, that shows you that your manifesting skills are working. Evaluate yourself not on how fast you get something, but on how satisfied you are by what you attract. Creating abundance will require that you let go of any remaining beliefs that money and objects are *hard* to create, because they aren't. You are now ready to begin creating a life you love, doing activities you love, and experiencing the joy of living in abundance.

PLAYSHEET

Below is a summary of the qualities that attract and repel money. Close your eyes and think of a number between 1 and 42. Refer to that number on the list below. For one day, work on developing the attracting quality of the pair below. If you notice yourself doing something that repels money, place a positive, attracting thought or action alongside the negative, repelling one.

Attracting qualities	Repelling qualities
1 | Honoring your worth and time	Not honoring your worth and time
2 | Giving and receiving freely	Not giving or being open to receive
3 | Opening your heart	Closing your heart
4 | Expecting the best to happen	Worrying that the worst will happen
5 | Coming from your heart	Getting into power struggles
6 | Doing your best	Cutting corners
7 | Wanting everyone to succeed, cooperating	Competing
8 | Focusing on how you can serve others	Thinking only of what others will give you
9 | Telling yourself why you can succeed	Telling yourself why you can't succeed
10 | Coming from your integrity	Compromising your values and ideals

Attracting qualities	Repelling qualities
11 | Being aware and paying attention	Operating on automatic
12 | Applauding others' success	Feeling threatened by others' success
13 | Embracing your challenges	Choosing safety and comfort over growth
14 | Releasing things easily	Hanging on to things
15 | Believing it's never too late, taking action on your dreams	Thinking it's too late, giving up
16 | Giving yourself permission to be and do what you want	Waiting for others to give you permission
17 | Believing your path is important	Not believing in your path
18 | Doing what you love for your livelihood	Working only for the money
19 | Detaching, surrendering to your higher good	Feeling needy or that you must have something
20 | Giving to other's prosperity	Giving to other's need
21 | Doing your higher purpose activities first	Putting off higher purpose activities until you have more time
22 | Seeing yourself as the source of your abundance	Viewing others as the source of your abundance

Attracting qualities	Repelling qualities
23 | Believing in abundance	Believing in scarcity
24 | Believing in yourself, self-confidence, self-love	Worrying, fears, doubts, self-criticism
25 | Clear intent and directed will	Vague or undefined goals
26 | Following your joy	Forcing yourself, creating "have tos" and "shoulds"
27 | Surrounding yourself with objects that reflect your aliveness	Keeping objects that aren't tools to express your aliveness
28 | Expressing gratitude and thanks	Feeling the world owes you
29 | Trusting in your ability to create abundance	Worrying over finances
30 | Following your inner guidance	Ignoring inner guidance
31 | Looking for a winning solution for everyone	Not caring if other person wins
32 | Becoming your own authority	Not believing in your inner wisdom
33 | Measuring abundance as fulfilling your purpose and happiness	Measuring abundance only by how much money you have
34 | Enjoying the process as much as the goal	Doing things only for the goal
35 | Clear agreements	Unspoken or vague expectations

Attracting qualities	Repelling qualities
36 | Thinking how far you have come	Focusing on how far you have to go
37 | Speaking of abundance	Talking about problems and lack
38 | Remembering past successes	Remembering past failures
39 | Thinking in expanded, unlimited ways	Thinking in limited ways
40 | Thinking of how you will *create* money	Focusing on how you *need* money
41 | Focusing on what you love and want	Focusing only on what you don't want
42 | Allowing yourself to have	Feeling you don't deserve

Acknowledgments

From our hearts we want to thank Orin and DaBen for their unending patience, guidance, and wisdom.

We want to thank our nieces and nephews whose love has taught us the true meaning of abundance: John, Elise, Mary, Tabatha, Justin, Heather, David, Erin, and DeeAnn. We also want to acknowledge our parents, Court and Shirley Smith and Glenn and Catherine Packer, who have taught us much about money and prosperity; and our brothers and sisters, Debra, Patricia, David, Robert, and Irene who have helped us see our beliefs about prosperity even more clearly.

We want to thank JoAnn Johnson, Gloria Dozier, and Georgia Schroer for their excellent management of the office that has given us the time to channel this book, as well as Mary Pat Mahan, Jeanie Cragin, and David Duty.

We want to extend our love and gratitude to those who helped us organize the guides' material and put it into this form: Elaine Ratner for her fine editing, Linda Merrill for her editing assistance, Greg Armstrong for his organizational help, Phillip Weber for his insights and ideas, and Judith Cornell for her outstanding artwork. We especially want to thank Hal and Linda Kramer and their guides for their friendship, love, support, and willingness to create new forms with us. We also want to thank our friends LaUna Huffines and Ed and Amerinda Alpern for being so generous with their love, time, and energy.

Companion Books by Orin and DaBen

Orin books:

Orin has put together a course called the Earth Life Series to assist you in learning to live with joy, becoming aware of the energy around you, and growing spiritually. This course is contained in several books. Each book is complete in itself and they can be read in any order.

The first book, *Living with Joy*, teaches you how to express your inner qualities of love, joy, well-being, and inner peace. To create money and abundance is to learn to radiate these qualities, for as you do you become more magnetic to the forms, objects, and greater flow of money that support your increased aliveness. In this book you will learn how to radiate love; increase your feelings of self-worth and self-esteem; and achieve more balance, stability, and security. You will learn to open to receive, take a quantum leap, gain clarity, open to new things, have inner peace, and have more freedom to be who you are and do what you want with your life. You will also learn about living in harmony with your higher purpose and discovering your life purpose. You will learn more about appreciation, gratitude, and the laws of increase; and how to change negative situations into positive ones. You will learn to live with joy rather than struggle.

The second book, *Personal Power Through Awareness*, will teach you how to become aware of the energies around you and follow your inner guidance. This is an accelerated, step-by-step course in sensing energy. Using these easy-to-follow processes, thousands have learned to create immediate and profound changes in their relationships, self-image, and ablity to love and be loved. You need no longer be affected by other people's moods or negativity. You can recognize when you have taken on other people's energies and easily release them. You can learn to stay centered and balanced, to know who you are, to increase the positive energy around you, and to love and help yourself and others. Your sensitivity is a gift. Learn to use it to send and receive telepathic messages, increase your intuitive abilities, and open to higher guidance. You can leave the denser energies, where things are often painful, and live in the higher energies where you can feel more loving, calm, focused, and positive.

The third book, *Spiritual Growth: Being Your Higher Self*, teaches you how to *be* your Higher Self, which knows unlimited abundance. You will learn how to link with the Universal Mind to turn what you want into energy and birth it into matter, align with the Higher Will to carry out your higher purpose, and play with light for healing and growth. You will learn how to lift the veils of illusion to see truth, expand and contract time, raise your vibration, achieve higher states of consciousness, open your heart, and know yourself in new, more loving ways. You will learn the skills of non-attachment, right use of will, being transparent to others' energies, and communicating as your Higher Self. You will learn to become a source of light and to grow through world service. This book offers you the next step in your spiritual growth for you who want to know more about who you are, why you are here, and what you came to do. You can align with the higher energies that are coming and use them to create the best life you can imagine for yourself.

BOOK I OF THE SOUL LIFE SERIES

Soul Love
Awakening Your Heart Centers

In *Soul Love*, Orin's first book of the Soul Life Series, you will meet and blend with your soul. You will learn more about your chakras and how to work with your soul and the Beings of Light to awaken your heart centers. When these centers are awakened and working together in a triangle of light, you can more easily experience soul love, peace, joy, bliss, and aliveness.

Discover how to attract a soul mate, soul link, make heart connections, create soul relationships, change personality love into soul love, and lift all the energies about you into your heart center to be purified and transformed. See results in your life when you use Orin's easy, step-by-step processes to heal your heart of past hurts, to open to receive more love, and to bring all your relationships to a higher level. (H J Kramer, Inc, 252 pages)

An Orin and DaBen book:

Opening to Channel: How to Connect With Your Guide
Creating money and abundance is easier when you link with your Higher Self, soul, or a high-level guide, receiving direct verbal guidance about your path and purpose. Channeling is a skill that can be learned. It is possible for you to connect with a spirit guide or your Higher Self, whether or not you have ever had any psychic experiences or have practiced meditation. This connection can help you create what you want more easily, and can help you find answers for everything from mundane everyday problems to the most challenging philosophical issues. You can learn to channel to bring through knowledge, personal guidance, philosophy, healing techniques, new business ideas, and much more. When you are ready, connecting with your guide or Higher Self will help to change your life for the better and to connect with your higher purpose.

Books

Living with Joy, by Sanaya Roman, channel for Orin. Keys to Personal Power and Spiritual Transformation. (H J Kramer Inc, 216 pages) *LWJ $12.95*

Personal Power Through Awareness, by Sanaya Roman, channel for Orin. A Guidebook for Sensitive People. (H J Kramer Inc, 216 pages) *PPTA $12.95*

Spiritual Growth: Being Your Higher Self, by Sanaya Roman, channel for Orin. (H J Kramer Inc, 252 pages) *SG $12.95*

Soul Love: *Awakening Your Heart Centers*, by Sanaya Roman, channel for Orin. Book I of the Soul Life Series. (H J Kramer Inc, 252 pages) *SL $12.95*

Opening to Channel: How to Connect With Your Guide, by Sanaya Roman and Duane Packer, channels for Orin and DaBen. (H J Kramer Inc, 264 pages) *OTC $12.95*

Call or write for a Free Subscription to our Newsletter:

To receive a FREE subscription to our newsletter with messages from Orin and DaBen on current earth changes, information on the energies present, and how to work with them, as well as information about tapes and seminars, write to *LuminEssence Productions*, P.O. Box 19117, Oakland, CA 94619, call (541) 770-6700, or visit our website at www.orindaben.com. Be sure to include your name, address, and phone number.

Our Best-Selling Audio Cassette Tape Course

Creating Money

Orin: I offer guided meditations to you who want to use and live the principles in this book. Working with guided meditations, where your mind is in a relaxed, open state is one of the most powerful ways known to create rapid, profound, and lasting changes in your life. Release subconscious programs that aren't bringing you what you want and replace them with higher ones. Create immediate results in your life as you open to your greater potential. These *Creating Money* tapes are guided meditations that will help you to reprogram your subconscious and increase your abundance potential. This album is the perfect companion to the book *Creating Money: Keys to Abundance.* Tapes may be purchased as singles (same journey on both sides), or as a tape album.

Magnetizing Yourself
You can learn to turn on your money "magnet" and draw in money and abundance. Align your actions with the spiritual laws of abundance. Reprogram at a cellular level for greater abundance. *SI010 $9.98*

Linking With Your Soul and the Guides
Work with a guide to create money and to fulfill your higher purpose. Meet and work with your soul which is always abundant. *SI076 $9.98*

Clearing Beliefs and Old Programs
This is a powerful and life-changing process to identify and release beliefs that are not working and establish new, positive ones. *SI071 $9.98*

Releasing Doubts and Fears
Become more powerful and confident, and let go of any fears that may be holding you back from having abundance. Believe in your unlimited capacity to create prosperity and anything you want. *SI075 $9.98*

Aura Clearing, Energy, and Lightwork
Work on the energy fields around your body to increase your vibration and become magnetic to all the forms, sums of money, and people that serve this new level. *SI073 $9.98*

Success!!
Release your fear of success or failure. Imagine success in every area of your life; go beyond previous limits, and create your dreams. *SI070 $9.98*

Abundance
This is a journey of learning to receive, believing you deserve, and opening to unlimited joy, love, and prosperity. *SI072 $9.98*

Awakening Your Prosperity Self
Talk with the part of you that creates your prosperity. Give it a new vision of who you are and what you want. One of the most powerful techniques known for creating positive changes in your life. *SI074 $9.98*

Buy All Eight Meditations and Save

The *Creating Money* tapes are $9.98 each if purchased separately. You can save by purchasing the entire set of four tapes (8 sides) for $49.95. Specify M100 on order form. Beautiful new age music by Thaddeus on all tapes. *(Free tape offer does not apply to albums.)* **M100** *$49.95*

Advanced Manifesting Seminar on Tape

This *Advanced Manifesting and Magnetizing* course by Orin and DaBen will teach you additional techniques for manifesting that go beyond what you have learned in this book. This *Advanced Manifesting* course (recorded at a live seminar) is for you who want to become skilled at manifesting, and want to manifest something in particular such as a house, car, new job, and so on. The results for people who have used these processes have been wonderful. You will learn how to manifest something you want by turning what you want into energy, bringing the energy of it into your DNA, utilizing the power of your emotions to draw it to you, and opening to receive what you want as you magnetize it to you. In addition, you will discover more about your life purpose, magnetize what you want, and reprogram at a cellular level for abundance. You will discover how to open to the unlimited abundance of your Higher Self, expand your consciousness, energize your life's work, and draw to you what you want. Set of four tapes (approximately four hours long) in cassette album. W005 $49.95 *(Free tape offer does not apply.)*

Get Your Work Out to the World
Orin Meditations

For Self-Employed People:
Attracting Business, Clients, Sales and Money
Magnetize business, see the higher purpose of your business, and link with your Higher Self and the higher forces of the universe to create a prosperous, successful business. *SI037 $9.98*

My Perfect Career
You will be guided to find a career that will give you joy, fulfillment, and a rewarding life-style. You will look at the essence of your perfect career, visualize and magnetize it, and allow it to come to you easily. *SI058 $9.98*

Discovering Your Life Purpose:
Why Am I Here? What Am I Here to Do?
You may feel you have something special to do but not yet know what it is. This will help you look at your life from a higher perspective, discover more about your path and what you came to accomplish. *L104 $9.98*

Manifesting Your Destiny
Contains many powerful processes to assist you in seeing why you are here and becoming magnetic to success. *SI009 $9.98*

Opening Creativity—Attracting Ideas
This will assist you in any creative endeavor you are undertaking—writing, music, art, and business. Ideas can flow after you go up to the Universal Mind, link with the Higher Will, and utilize the power of your Higher Self. *SI046 $9.98*

Public Recognition
Magnetize people to your work and prepare to handle having more and more people connect with you through your work. *SI015 $9.98*

Note: Above single audio cassette tapes contain the same journey on both sides and beautiful music by Thaddeus. For information on additional guided meditations, write or call *LuminEssence Productions.*

Audiocassette Tape Courses by Orin

Solar Radiance
Becoming a More Perfect Light

This course in working with light is also an advanced course in manifesting. In it, you will learn how to work with the Solar light, one of the most powerful forces in the universe. Your vision of what is possible in your life can expand and you can know what steps to take to create what you want. You can manifest those forms that hold the most light for you. You will experience how creation of matter and form comes about from the world of light into your world of form. You will work with translating this light from the Universal Mind to your higher mind and intellect, so you can know what actions to take to bring about what you want.

Side 1: Increasing Your Radiance: Expand your consciousness and align with the Solar light to become a more radiant and perfect light.

Side 2: Transforming Your Life with Light: Work with the qualities of Solar light to transform any circumstance, situation, habit, or blockage.

Side 3: Creating More Light About You: View the people and situations in your life from a higher level and add light to them.

Side 4: Birthing Light and Awareness: Find your next steps and discover new ideas, directions, and answers, including what is next in creating your life purpose and your path of enlightenment.

Side 5: Becoming a More Perfect Light: Work with three Masters who will transmit Solar light and energy to you to expand your ability to align with the Higher Will, and to express the creative intelligence within you.

Side 6: Liberating the Light Within: Release old thoughts, beliefs, dense emotions, and old patterns to become more aware of your inner guidance.

Side 7: Condensing Light Into Matter—Manifesting With Light: Find those things you want to manifest as they exist as light in the higher dimensions, add Solar light to them, and condense this light into matter.

Side 8: Building a Solar Consciousness: With a Solar consciousness you can learn to find and use the light in every moment.

Set of four tapes (eight journeys) in attractive album. Beautiful music by Thaddeus. *SL104 $49.95*

Becoming a Writer

Side 1: I Am a Writer: Visualize yourself as a successful writer. Create new beliefs about your ability to write and succeed with your writing.

Side 2: Manifesting Your Writing: Using advanced manifesting techniques, you will connect with the Universal Mind, work with your book or project as energy, birth it into matter in its highest form, harmonize with it, and open to receive your success.

Side 3: Loving to Write: You will get in touch with your higher vision, deeper wisdom, and higher purpose. This will inspire you to write, get started, move through any blocks, and be creative.

Side 4: Connecting With Your Audience: You will reach through time and space and connect with the people who will be assisted by your writing, generating energy around your work so your books/projects will succeed. You will magnetize a publisher/producer for your work.

Set of two tapes (four meditations) in attractive album. Tapes contain beautiful music by Thaddeus. *(Individual tapes not sold separately. Free tape offer does not apply to albums.) SI016 $29.95*

Affirmation Cards
For a Daily Abundance Message

We have made available the affirmations that appear in the *Creating Money* book as calling-card size cards you can carry with you. Choose a card every day and use that affirmation as a message from your Higher Self about the area you can work on to increase your abundance. 112 blue linen cards in attractive box. *CMA $12.95*

Audiocassette Guided Meditations by Orin

Abundance Affirmations/General Magnetism: Made to accompany the *Creating Money* book. Side 1 of this audio cassette tape contains all of the affirmations from the *Creating Money* book. Side 2 includes the powerful magnetizing technique from the *Creating Money* book which you can use to draw to yourself money, small and large objects, and anything else you want. *M001 $9.98*

Unlimited Thinking: Link with your soul to expand your vision of what you can have. Expand your thinking to release limits. *SI108 $9.98*

Open to Receive: Allow things to come easily to you, open your heart, and believe you deserve to have what you want. *L106 $9.98*

Clearing Blockages: If you have an intolerable situation or an issue you can't solve, use this to change your circumstances. *SI057 $9.98*

Meeting Your Spirit Guide: This is a beginning journey to sense, see, or hear your guide and receive guidance and advice. *014 $9.98*

Being Your Higher Self: Become your Higher Self, view your life from this higher perspective, and give yourself advice. *SI040 $9.98*

Opening Up All Your Psychic Abilities: Processes to help you awaken your psychic abilities. *013 $9.98*

Developing Intuition: Following your intuition can save you hours of work, lead you to opportunities and help you find answers. *010 $9.98*

Self-Love: Learn to love and nurture yourself, to release things that are not loving to you, and to create new, positive beliefs. *L102 $9.98*

Attracting Your Soul-Mate: You will be guided to meet your soul-mate telepathically, then draw him or her into your life. *RE002 $9.98*

Losing Weight, Looking Younger: Build finer matter into your body, build cellular radiance, and lose weight. *SI030 $9.98*

Radiating Unconditional Love: As you increase love in your life, you become magnetic to people, success, and abundance. *P103 $9.98*

Reprogramming at Cellular Level: Change your life by reprogramming your DNA to achieve your goals and dreams. *SI056 $9.98*

Note: Above single audio cassette tapes contain the same journey on both sides and beautiful music by Thaddeus. For information on additional guided meditations, write or call *LuminEssence Productions*.

Call or write for a Free Subscription to our Newsletter

To receive a FREE subscription to our newsletter with messages from Orin and DaBen as well as information about new tapes and seminars write to *LuminEssence Productions*, P.O. Box 19117, Oakland, CA 94619, call (541) 770-6700, or visit our website at www.orindaben.com. Be sure to include your name, address, and phone number.

LuminEssence Productions • P.O. Box 19117 • Oakland, CA 94619
To order by phone with Visa/Mastercard call (541) 770-6700
www.orindaben.com

Order Form

BUY THREE $9.98 TAPES AND GET A FOURTH $9.98 TAPE FREE!!
(Free tape offer does not apply to tape albums.)

Your Name _____
(Please print)

Address _____

City_____ State _____ Zip _____

Country _____

Telephone: Home (_____)_____ Work (_____)_____
(Telephone required by shippers for international shipments.)

QTY	ITEM	DESCRIPTION	PRICE

Shipping and Handling Subtotal:	**U.S.A.** First Class Mail	U.P.S.	**International Air Mail** Canada	Europe	Other International	
Up to $10 ...	$2.75	$4.60	$3.75	$5.70	$6.90	Subtotal
$11 to $50 ...	$4.15	$5.10	$7.30	$11.00	$14.50	Shipping
$51 to $89 ...	$5.50	$5.50	$8.30	$13.65	$18.85	TOTAL
$90 to $100 ...	$7.05	$6.95	$9.55	$19.80	$24.35	
$101 to $200 ...	$8.30	$8.10	$14.60	$28.90	$39.90	*Thank You*
Over $200 ...	$10.75	$9.45	$19.30	$47.00	$56.65	*for*

☐ Check here if you prefer your order shipped UPS.
(UPS cannot deliver to PO Box addresses.)

Your Order!

Payment enclosed: ☐ Check   ☐ Money Order

Please charge my: ☐ Visa   ☐ Mastercard

Credit Card No. _____ Exp. Date _____

Signature as on card _____

Please make check payable to **LuminEssence Productions**. Remember to allow time for U.S. Mail or UPS delivery after order is shipped. All orders shipped within two business days of receipt. Incomplete orders will be returned. **International orders** payable in U.S. Funds drawn ON a U.S. bank. All international orders will be shipped by air mail. For international orders, we prefer payment by credit card if possible.   M12

Awakening Your Light Body
Keys to Enlightenment

Awakening Your Light Body will be Orin and DaBen's next book. It is available now as an audio cassette tape course with extensive written material. What is your light body? What will understanding, using, and attuning to your light body do for you? As your light body awakens, you draw to yourself opportunities to make a difference in the world. Awakening your light body can assist you in having a clearer vision of what you are here to do, lifting the veils so you can see more of your purpose and who you are. If you are teaching or working with others, it will help your work to have a more profound effect and to make you more magnetic to clients and students. Awakening your light body can help you create states of inner illumination, mental clarity, and an open heart. You can more easily choose how you want to feel and the thoughts you want to have. You will be more focused, mentally alert, and physically vibrant. Call or write to *LuminEssence* for a newsletter containing complete information on this six-volume tape course.

Join Orin and DaBen for Sunday Morning Meditations

Many of you throughout the world are reading and studying Orin and DaBen's work. We want to thank all of you for your support of their work, and offer you an opportunity to continue our connection by inviting you to join Orin and DaBen on the inner planes on Sunday mornings. We meditate and focus light upon you if you ask for it and are open to receive it. Experience the light and transformation that is possible as thousands meditate together on the inner planes. Deepen your connection to the Beings of Light and other lightworkers as you join us. Orin and DaBen will transmit to all of you who join us on Sunday mornings from 9:00 to 9:30 AM, California time. (Or, join us at 9:00 to 9:30 your time and we will create light together that will move around the world.) For more information about how to join us see our newsletter.

Join us for our Worldwide
Orin and DaBen Meditations

We have global linkups at least once a year to call upon the Great Ones to assist humanity. Thousands join us on the inner planes to be a point of light to call upon and receive energy from the Great Ones, and then to radiate that energy to humanity. In the past we have called upon the Great Ones to assist us in awakening our heart centers, changing thoughts of scarcity into abundance, and to grow through joy and release struggle and pain. In addition, you can join us on the inner planes during our regular Sunday morning meditations. You can ask to receive energy from DaBen and Orin, experience the power of thousands meditating together, and transform your life in any area you focus on. Write to us for a free subscription to our newsletter containing information about the next global linkup and about our Sunday morning Orin and DaBen meditations.